PALS-1

SITE ASSESSMENT

for Better Gardens and Landscapes

Charles P. Mazza

PALS-1
October 2013

© 2013 by PALS (Plant and Life Sciences Publishing)
All rights reserved. Inquiries invited.

ISBN-13: 978-1-933395-30-2

Request to reprint parts of this book should be sent to PALS.
In your request, please state which parts of the book you would
like to reprint and describe how you intend to use the material.
Contact PALS if you have any questions.

Plant and Life Sciences Publishing (PALS)
PO Box 4557
Ithaca, NY 14852- 4557
phone: (607) 255-7654 • fax (607) 254-8770
e-mail: PALSPUBLISHING@CORNELL.EDU
website: HTTP://PALSPUBLISHING.CALS.CORNELL.EDU/

Library of Congress Cataloging-in-Publication Data

Mazza, Charles P.
Site assessment for better gardens and landscapes / Charles P. Mazza.
    p. cm.
Summary: "Provides information on assessing the characteristics of a
site to develop a sustainable landscape or garden design"--Provided by
publisher.
Includes bibliographical references and index.
ISBN 978-1-933395-30-2 (pbk.)
1. Gardens--Design. 2. Landscape design. I. Title.
SB473.M32 2013
635.9--dc23
                                                      2013031283

Printed October 2013

On the cover

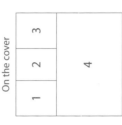

1	2	3
	4	

1. Bud scar on a red horsechestnut tree. (source: Susan Day)

2. The author and a master gardener harvest Chinese
   long beans at a New York City community garden.
   (source: Lisa Miller)

3. Measuring the circumference of a tree to determine
   the diameter. (source: Author)

4. Chipmunk on a garden wall. (source: Author)

Contents

Activities and Sidebars

iv

About the Author

Charles P. Mazza is the former statewide leader in the home-grounds and community horticulture extension program, including the Master Gardener Program, in the Department of Horticulture at Cornell University. In the department, he taught a horticultural problem-solving course for undergraduates, was a frequent lecturer in other horticultural undergraduate courses, and taught an online course in organic gardening for North America. He led the urban horticulture program for Cornell Cooperative Extension in New York City, was the assistant to the director and later headed the education program for youth and adults at Brooklyn Botanic Garden, and served on the board of Green Guerillas, a community garden activist group in New York City. His career spanned four decades. He designed and cared for gardens in New York, New Jersey, Connecticut, Pennsylvania, and Virginia. He received a B.A. degree from Franklin and Marshall College in biology/ botany, an M.S. degree in horticulture from Rutgers University and an M.P.A. degree from New York University. While retired from Cornell University, he is still active. He volunteers at Burnside Plantation, an historic farm in Pennsylvania, and gives educational tours at the Morris Arboretum in Philadelphia.

Acknowledgments

The following people and organizations assisted with the development of this book: Nina Bassuk, Lori Brewer, Marc Circeo, Michael Circeo, Cornell University Library, Craig Cramer, Paul Curtis, Delaware Valley College Library, Marcia Eames-Sheavly, Kenneth Harbison, Susan Henninger, Ruth McMaken, Marvin Pritts, Tammo Steenhuis, Susan Thompson, Richard Uva, Christopher Watkins, and Wendy Wirth.

Several people reviewed earlier versions of the book and their comments were helpful. In 2006 and 2007, forty-one Master Gardeners from New York State (Ontario, Chemung, Orleans, Washington, and Rensselaer Counties) field-tested and critiqued an earlier version of this book. The manuscript was peer reviewed by several professionals from Ohio, Rhode Island, West Virginia, New York, Tennessee, New Jersey, Massachusetts and Connecticut.

Marty Sailus, PALS Director, managed the publication and provided developmental editing and copyediting. Holly Hyde, former PALS editor, organized the 2007 peer review and copyedited an earlier version of the manuscript.

All photos by Charles P. Mazza, unless indicated above the photo on the right. Some photos indicate HGIC as the source. This stands for Home and Garden Information Center, University of Maryland. Illustrations of Pete and Herb were drawn by Derik R. Diaz, except the drawing on page 41 was drawn by Jeffrey Miller.

The following organizations, businesses, and individuals provided photograph locations and assistance: Naalamle Amissah, Obdulia Baltazar, Charlie Blackmer, Burnside Plantation, Community Gardens in Manhattan and Brooklyn, Cornell Plantations, Cornell University campus, Frelinghuysen Aboretum,Pamela Hudak, Helen Keith, Lakeside Nursing Home, Adele Lopatin, Mazza Hair Center, Morris Arboretum, Park Place Association, Wave Hill, and Marie Wilcox. Additional photos were taken at various locations in New York State and Pennsylvania.

Initial Funding for this project was provided by Cornell Cooperative Extension and New York State Integrated Pest Management Program.

Plant and Life Sciences Publishing (PALS) is a program of the Department of Horticulture, in the College of Agriculture and Life Sciences, at Cornell University.

v

General Planning Information

Assessing a property is the first step in creating a new garden or landscape—or giving an old one a facelift. Most property owners don't know how to do it right, so it is often overlooked or short changed. The assessment involves collecting detailed information about the property's characteristics and its ability to support healthy plant growth. This step-by-step workbook is designed to help prevent unnecessary plant replacement and labor costs through careful site assessment. If you are new to gardening and landscaping, review the glossary to become familiar with common horticultural terms used in this workbook.

Since site assessment puts you in partnership with the environment, it results in a sustainable and easy-to-care-for landscape or garden. It reveals the limitations and opportunities to support plant growth. Plants experience stress when their oxygen, water, light, nutrient, carbon dioxide, and temperature requirements are not met. Site assessment allows you to account for these factors when designing your landscape or garden.

Site assessment is a discovery process. Completing the tasks described in this book will assist you in:

- Selecting appropriate plants for the site
- Minimizing plant disease problems
- Saving money
- Identifying conditions that lead to plant stress
- Developing strategies for improving the site

Is site assessment something that has to be done to have a successful landscape or garden? Yes, although there are probably examples of success without a site assessment. If you discover a factor in the site assessment, you cope better with it and make an informed decision.

Should the assessment be done only for perennial herbaceous and woody plants, or should it be done for fruits, lawns, annual flowers, herbs, and vegetables? Do an assessment for all parts of your garden and landscape—on any size property or section of it, regardless of what you are planting.

Can it be done only on a part of the property? You can focus on part(s) of the property, referred to as study areas in this book. Keep in

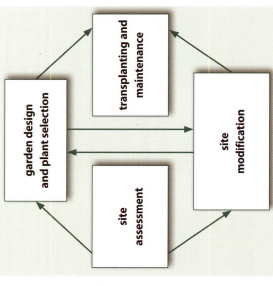

Site assessment precedes garden design, plant selection, site modification, and transplanting/maintenance.

source: Lisa Miller

Gardens can contain bulbs, annuals, perennials, vegetables, fruit, woody vines, trees, and shrubs.

mind that some of the physical factors you will discover about your garden are not restricted to one section alone. It is better to do an overall site assessment, but if your goals are to develop or improve one area, then assessing that area makes sense.

Can it be done in a community garden?

Discoveries made during the site assessment process are as useful in a community garden as they are in a private garden or landscape. Include community members in the assessment and in making a to-do list as described in Taking the Next Steps beginning on page 60.

Are there special considerations for gardens in urban areas?

Sites in urban areas where buildings have been demolished, along roads with heavy traffic, or on former industrial sites may have soils contaminated with heavy metals. Special soil tests are needed to determine if heavy metals are in soil. If you have concerns about heavy metals, arrange for a soil test, especially if you plan to grow food.

How can the assessment help to minimize plant diseases?

Stress factors make plants more vulnerable to disease. For instance, lack of oxygen in compacted, poorly drained soil stresses plants and makes disease organisms more likely to develop. Many plants set into damp, shady sites are more susceptible to diseases. Some plants are highly susceptible to diseases and others are more likely to have insect problems. The site assessment will help you choose plantings that are suited to the site such as insect-resistant or disease-resistant plants.

The author and a master gardener harvest Chinese long beans at a New York City community garden.

How should I pace the project? You can do it in short periods of time over a few weeks or spread the steps out over six months to a year so that you are doing one or two steps a month. Estimated time is included with the description of each step. It takes around eight hours and about 30 tools—

2

mostly inexpensive household items—to do all the steps in a site assessment.

If you stretch out the site assessment over a 6- to 12-month period, do most of it during the growing season. Step 2 (Obstructions Above and Below), Step 4 (Hardiness and Microclimates), Step 9 (Slope), Step 12 (Putting It All Together) and Taking the Next Steps can be done in the winter months. Of course, you can only "put it all together" or "take the next steps" after you have completed the activities and collected the information in Steps 1 through 11.

When should it be done? Do a site assessment before gardening or landscaping on a newly acquired property, before expanding into a new part of the property, or before refurbishing an older section. The site assessment will be helpful if you have had your property for several years but have not considered garden or landscape improvements. The site assessment will help a professional landscaper come up with a good plan for your property.

How do I use this workbook to conduct a site assessment? Each of the first 11 steps in this workbook has at least one activity that will improve your understanding of the site's limitations and opportunities. In Step 12, Putting It All Together, the knowledge gained through the site assessment will be summarized in one or more

Site Assessment Checklists (see page 59). Then in Taking the Next Steps, you will list your long term goals for the site, develop a landscape and garden design, and make a to-do list to implement the design.

Throughout the book plants are mentioned along with information on their tolerance of various conditions. You may consider these plants for your site and want more information. So, at the end of each step, there is a list of plants mentioned

Choosing a Site Assessment Notebook

Throughout this workbook, you are asked to record observations, information, calculations, and test results in a "site assessment notebook," sometimes referred to simply as "your notebook." In the last section, Taking the Next Steps, you will make several lists, including a to-do list that will be added to your notebook. Throughout the workbook, there are suggestions for further reading including books and web sites. And, you may seek advice from advisors and organizations mentioned in this book. Your notebook will be used to keep all the information discovered in one place. Before starting the assessment, decide what type of notebook you will use, paper or digital or both.

If you decide to use a paper notebook, choose a spiral-bound notebook about the same size as this book. Spiral binding allows the book to lay flat on any page. So it is easier to make notes and sketches. Consider adding tabs to mark the beginning of notes for

each step. Then, you can easily turn to the notes section for a step when new information becomes available.

Build the notebook as you work through the steps in the assessment. Date your entries. When you are finished with a step, leave some blank pages at the end for additional information from advisors, reference books, and web sites.

If you decide to keep your notes on a digital storage device, start by setting up a folder for each of the twelve steps and Taking the Next Steps. A digital notebook allows you to use software to make tables and it is easier to make changes as more information becomes available.

You may decide to have a paper and digital component to your notebook. You can use a paper notebook for notes, but store photos on a digital storage device. Spreadsheet software can be used for lists and test results.

in the step. The list includes the common name and scientific name. The scientific name will make it easier to research additional information on the plant and to locate it in a nursery. Scientific names include two words, a *Genus* and a *species* in an italic font. The first letter of the genus is capitalized. If there is more than one species appropriate to how it is used in the text, "sp." will indicate multiple species for the genus. An "x" in the scientific name indicates it is a hybrid.

At the end of each step, look for a list of books and websites for further reading. Starting on page 69 there is a comprehensive list of references and resources. The list is divided into four sections: General Advice, Landscape Design, Plant Selection, and Growing Vegetables and Fruits. When you explore websites or books, record information or reminders in your site assessment notebook. Books and websites will provide information about a plant that can help you determine if it will thrive at a location.

If you are new to gardening, some terms used in this workbook may not be familiar. If you see an unfamiliar term, check the extensive glossary starting on page 71 for a definition.

What do I do when my assessment suggests that I make a change? In the Taking the Next Steps, after you have completed the site assess-ment, you will prioritize changes in a to-do list that includes a completion date for making each change. Some changes are simple and can be done in a few hours at low cost. Other changes involve significant planning, time, and money to do effectively; those can be done later. Make it a priority to fix unsafe conditions in frequently used areas.

Where do I get advice, if I need it? Throughout the book, sources of advice are mentioned including local Cooperative Extension offices. Cooperative Extension may be a good source of information on local climate, plants that thrive in the area, soil testing labs, gardening classes, and state-level horticulture experts. Cooperative Extension is a nationwide education system that originally had offices in each U.S. county. In some states, multi-county Extension offices have replaced county offices. Local offices are linked to the state's land grant university. Some states have local gardening education programs supported by horticultural experts at the state's land grant university. Other states may not offer this service.

Utility companies provide information on underground conduits and overhead wires. Soil and Water Conservation Districts provide information on local soils and wetland rules if needed. Using the books and websites mentioned in this book, you can find information on all aspects of land-scapes and gardens. Landscape architects can be good consultants for problem areas.

If there is a public garden (botanic(al) garden, arboretum) in your area, check to see if they provide gardening advice, particularly on the environmental needs of plants or questions about existing plants. Visiting a public garden may help you visualize your landscape and garden goals, especially the plants you want to include.

Neighbors may be a source of advice but you will need to differentiate between opinions and good information. They are a source of information on factors the neighborhood shares, like wind and roaming animals.

PETE AND HERB

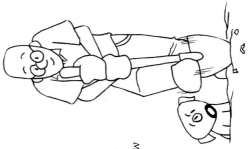

Throughout the workbook, you will see drawings of Pete and his dog, Herb, doing activities on their newly acquired property. Follow the adventures of Pete and Herb as they assess their property.

PLANT MENTIONED IN THIS SECTION

The common name is followed by the scientific name and then additional information if needed.

Chinese long beans – *Vigna unguiculata sesquipedalis*

In this scientific name, the third name is the subspecies.

FOR FURTHER READING

Visit **http://www.hort.cornell.edu/site/** *for a link to the web sites below and all web sites mentioned in this book.*

Botanical Gardens, Public Gardens, and Arboretum Locations

http://gardenvisit.com/gardens/in/usa

From Nightingale Garden Company, Ltd., registered in England and Wales.

http://www.garden.org/public_garden

From the National Gardening Association.

Cooperative Extension Office Locations

http://www.csrees.usda.gov/Extension/

From the United States Department of Agriculture.

Home and Garden Information Center

http://www.extension.umd.edu/hgic

Horticultural information to the public nationwide through a diagnostic website. Sponsored by the University of Maryland Cooperative Extension.

Information about Heavy Metals

http://www.uvm.edu/vtvegandberry/factsheets/interpreting_heavy_metals_soil_tests.pdf

From the University of Vermont, by Vern Grubinger and Don Ross

https://sites.google.com/site/healthygardeners/

Information about heavy metals and gardening. Produced by Jennifer Gorospe, San José State University as part of her Master's Thesis.

http://www.gardening.cornell.edu/factsheets/misc/cgandlead.html

Information about children, gardens, and lead, by Linda M. Ameroso and Charles P. Mazza, Cornell Cooperative Extension, NYC.

Garden and Landscape Area

WHY IS THIS IMPORTANT?

Knowing the area of your garden or landscape is useful when making decisions. The square footage is needed to purchase materials, including grass seed, fertilizer, compost, and mulch. It is also used to determine the number of plants needed to cover an area.

Knowing the dimensions of sections of your property, such as lawn areas, an alcove, or an extra area in an odd-shaped property will be helpful. The success of landscape or garden plans depends on accurate information to match the layout with the realities of the site size. For instance, an ornamental tree that matures within the boundaries of the available space will save replacement or pruning costs. Fruit trees come in many different sizes depending on the rootstock used. They need extra space for air circulation to minimize disease, to maintain the tree, and to harvest fruit. Knowing the area of a vegetable garden is useful when purchasing mulch, compost, plants, and other materials.

It is important to know the location of water outlets (usually faucets on the outside of the house), electrical outlets (for using power equipment outdoors), existing pathways, especially permanent ones, and unsafe areas. This information is essential to successful planning.

ACTIVITY

Start a property sketch.

MATERIALS

- Retractable 25', 50' or 100' measuring tape, or yardstick
- paper, letter or legal size, preferably grid lined
- Property survey
- Pencil
- Clipboard
- Site assessment notebook

ESTIMATED TIME: 1 hour

Find your property survey, part of the deed to the property. Get the overall length and width of the property from the property survey. Draw a sketch of the property to scale as if you were looking at the site from an airplane. For example, the scale of the property survey shown on the next page is 1 inch equals 50 feet. Choose a scale that allows you to fit the sketch on the paper you are using. For large properties, use more than one sheet, but clearly mark how they fit together. Grid-lined paper makes it easy to draw areas to scale and is available at office supply stores.

You don't need to be a good artist to add the house, outbuildings, fences, walls, ponds, and other features to your sketch at their approximate size and location. Also, mark the location of permanent pathways, patios, driveways, electrical

Pete draws the property boundaries to scale on his sketch.

6

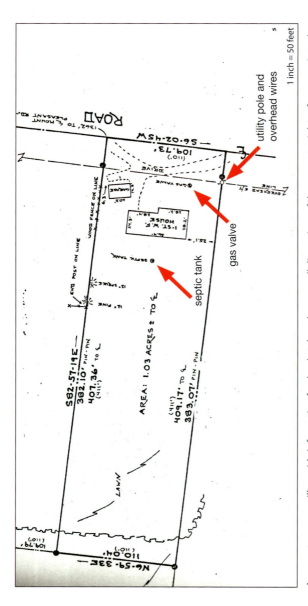

septic tank

gas valve

utility pole and
overhead wires

1 inch = 50 feet

A property survey will provide information for the sketch such as overall dimensions of the property, rights of way, septic tank location, overhead wires, and gas lines.

outlets, and hose outlets or other water sources.

Use the retractable measuring tape or yardstick to measure areas within the property. If part of the property is wooded or natural meadowland, measure the area that is currently used for lawns, landscapes, and gardens. The property survey may have some of this information. Measure undeveloped areas as well. The undeveloped areas can be considered for new garden, landscape or lawn areas.

When an area is too large to be measured with a measuring tape or yardstick, use the length of your average step. Use what ever is handy to mark the beginning and end of a straight line 20 feet long. The average length of your step is 20 feet divided by the number of steps it takes you to walk the distance. Now, count the number of steps it takes to walk the area's length and multiply it by your average step length. Do the same for the area width. Measuring your pace step gives you an estimate, not an exact measurement.

In the sidebar below, it is suggested that you add an "H" to the sketch to note the location of a hazardous area. In later steps you will be asked to add other letter codes. At the bottom of the sketch, leave a generous amount of space for a legend—an explanation of the codes. It will make it easier to interpret the sketch when you are finished.

On large properties, use more than one grid sheet, but clearly mark how they all fit together. Large grid sheets are available but may be harder to photocopy.

In addition to measuring currently used areas, measure undeveloped areas. The undeveloped areas can be considered for expansion of new garden, landscape or lawn areas.

USING WHAT YOU FOUND IN THIS STEP

Mark all the dimensions on the sketch and store the sketch on a clipboard. You will be asked to make notes on it in the steps that follow.

Convert length and width measurements for the whole or sections of your garden to square footage and mark it on your sketch.

Length (ft.) × width (ft.) = square feet

For areas that are not rectangular, imagine a rectangle around the space and calculate the area of the rectangle. Then, estimate the percentage of the rectangle that is occupied by the irregular shape. Multiply this percent by the area of the rectangle.

This will yield an estimate of the area of the irregular area. If you have some knowledge of geometry, you may want to estimate areas using circles, partial circles, and triangles as well as rectangles. Record your calculations in your notebook.

Supplies are ordered, based on square footage. For instance, if you want to cover an area with

3 inches of mulch, multiply the calculated square footage of the area by 0.25 feet (3 inches is 0.25 ft.) to get cubic feet. Divide this number by 27 to get cubic yards of mulch needed. There are 27 cubic feet per cubic yard.

New gardens, such as vegetable gardens, will require frequent watering. If the preferred space is more than 50 feet from a water outlet, arrange for a new outlet near the new garden. Water is essential to a garden and is too heavy to haul. Consider installing at least one outdoor electric outlet.

Existing paths will factor into future plans. Consider them in any decisions you make on garden design. Remove them if they are a safety hazard or if they interfere with your plans.

PLANT MENTIONED IN STEP 1

The common name is followed by the scientific name and then additional information if needed.

Poison ivy – *Rhus radicans*

FOR FURTHER READING

Wasp and Bee Management: A Common Sense Approach, NRAES-185, Jody Gangloff-Kaufmann, NRAES, Ithaca, NY, 2011. Purchase online at **http://palspublishing.cals.cornell.edu/**

Are There Unsafe Spots on Your Property?

This mature poison-ivy vine, with its characteristic three-leaflet groups and "hairy" stems (hugging the tree trunk), reach 30 to 40 feet into the canopy. It causes dermatitis to sensitive people and birds easily spread its seeds.

Unsafe spots put your family and guests at risk for injury. Examples of unsafe spots include:

- uneven spots in a patio, driveway, or walkway
- depressions or holes in the ground
- short, broken pipes or other obstructions sticking up from the ground
- nests of stinging insects (wasps, yellow jackets, and hornets), especially underground nests.
- trees with rotting or broken limbs
- poison ivy patches and vines

Look for places on your property that may be hazardous. Mark their location on the sketch with an H for hazard. Or, you can be more specific, for example, PI for poison ivy. Add the code and what it stands for to the sketch's legend. Add new unsafe spots to the sketch as you discover them.

If an unsafe spot is located in an area frequented by people, give it immediate attention. If it is located in an area not used regularly, it can be mitigated if you expand into the area.

Obstructions Above and Below

WHY IS THIS IMPORTANT?

As trees and shrubs mature they need ample room for their limbs and vast network of roots. When planting a new tree or shrub, consider its size at maturity. Before digging or planting, know the location of overhead utility wires, underground pipes, and conduits, and other possible obstructions. Water pipes, gas lines, cable TV lines, Internet lines, electrical conduits, and drain pipes may be underground. Local ordinances often favor the utilities, not trees. It is easier to avoid a conflict than it is to remedy the situation a decade or more after planting.

ACTIVITY

Where are the underground lines and overhead wires?

MATERIALS

- Sketch from Step 1
- Pencil
- Property survey
- Camera
- Site assessment notebook

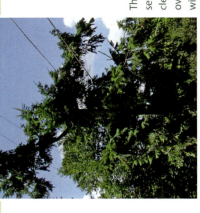

The tree is severely cut to clear the way for overhead utility wires.

ESTIMATED TIME: 30–45 minutes

This activity is quite easy. Most you can do yourself, one requires a visit from the utility company.

- Refer to your property survey for the location of sewer lines or the septic system. The property survey may also indicate the location of a well or incoming water lines. Add all of these to the property sketch. A septic system includes a tank and wide underground leach field.

- Indicate the location of heat and dryer vents on your sketch. When you make a landscape plan, be sure the vents will not be obstructed.

- There may also be legal considerations. On your sketch, locate any county, municipal, or utility rights-of-way, emergency access lanes that must be kept clear, and signs that must be readable from the road.

- Determine the location of underground wires and pipes by contacting your local utility company (gas and electric). Before any excavation is done, most utility companies will come to the property and install small colored flags above utility lines. The color indicates the type of underground conduit or pipe. Indicate the location of underground pipes and wires on your sketch. Photograph the area with flags to remind you of their location and add the photo to your notebook. The flags will not be permanent.

- Indicate the location of overhead wires that are on or near the property on the sketch. Estimate the height of the wires and record them in your notebook.

Using What You Found in this Step

If you find that aboveground wires run through your property, avoid planting trees and tall shrubs under them. You could choose trees whose mature height is lower than the wires. Planting trees that interfere with aboveground wires is costly; ultimately the tree is removed or disfigured by heavy pruning.

Examples of ornamental trees less than 30 feet high at maturity are cornelian cherry dogwood, crabapple, goldenrain tree, and American hornbeam. There are also dwarf and semi-dwarf fruit trees.

Trees that grow into or around aboveground wires pose a safety hazard in ice storms or other weather events. A utility company will prune in a right-of-way, but often without considering aesthetics. There may come a time when you have to excavate for repair or replacement of underground utilities. Removing trees can be costly.

Plant only grass or other shallow-rooted plants in the vicinity of the underground utilities. Trees may be planted ten feet from underground pipes. Weeping willow tree roots are notorious for invading sewer and water pipes; plant them in open areas without underground pipes. Plant shrubs at least two feet from pipes. Shallow-rooted perennials can be planted closer, since they are easily

A hand-drawn property sketch showing boundaries, obstructions, and more.

moved if necessary. Lawn grasses can be planted over a septic tank and leach field.

Utility wires cross near the top of the goldenrain tree. The tree has reached its mature height so there is little risk it will interfere with the wires.

PLANTS MENTIONED IN STEP 2

The common name is followed by the scientific name and then additional information if needed.

American hornbeam – *Carpinus caroliniana*. Other common names include ironwood, blue beech, or musclewood.

Ash – *Fraxinus* sp. – a genus of about 50 species, about 6 of which are common in North America.

Cornelian cherry dogwood – *Cornus mas*

Crabapple – *Malus* sp. There are at least six species and many more cultivars.

Goldenrain tree – *Koelreuteria paniculata*

Weeping willow – *Salix babylonica*

FOR FURTHER READING

Visit **http://www.hort.cornell.edu/site/** *for links to the web sites below and all web sites mentioned in this book.*

Dig-Safe System

www.digsafe.com/how_it_works.php

For residents of Maine, New Hampshire, Vermont, Rhode Island, and Massachusetts.

Dwarf and Semi-dwarf Fruit Trees

www.gardening.cornell.edu/fruit/homefruit/3treefruit.pdf

Options are explained in the tree fruit chapter of the *Cornell Guide to Growing Fruit at Home*, Cornell University, 2003.

Small Trees (less than 30')

www.hort.cornell.edu/uhi/outreach/recurbtree/pdfs/07~smalltrees.pdf

An extensive list of trees whose mature height is lower than the expected height of power lines. From *Recommended Urban Trees: Site Assessment and Tree Selection for Stress Tolerance*, Urban Horticulture Institute, Cornell University, 2009.

The mature crabapple tree (right) will not interfere with overhead utility wires. The ash tree about 50 feet behind and on the left was planted at the same time. It's mature height would interfere with overhead utility wires.

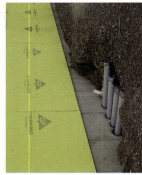

In new construction, conduits holding wires and cables exit the structure underground.

Irrigation Systems

Note the presence of an irrigation system with underground pipes. In your notebook, record if the water is delivered by sprinkler, drip (trickle), or micro-sprinkler/sprayer. Sprinklers that pop-up when the system is turned on are often used on turf where climate requires irrigation. Drip irrigation delivers water directly to the plant base through above ground or below ground emitters. When drip systems are not practical, such as for ground covers, micro-sprinklers are used. Micro-sprinklers cover a wider area than drip emitters.

If the use of an area is changed, the irrigation system may need to be removed and a new one installed if the new use warrants it. Consult an irrigation professional if changes are made and for system maintenance advice.

Here are some things you can do to get familiar with the irrigation system. Record calculations and observations in your notebook.

- Look for a system design or the system installer. The system design would show underground pipes and include specifications for sprinklers or emitters. Installers often put decals with contact information on the controller or other system component. The system design or installer is a good place to start for more information about the system.

- Locate underground pipes and show them on the sketch started in Step 1. Start by locating the system's connection to the water supply, usually under the house, in the basement, or on the main water line in the yard. Just after the connection, look for a brass backflow-prevention device. The device prevents water flow from the irrigation line into the drinking water and is required by most jurisdictions. For automatic systems, there will be a controller that turns the system on and off. After finding the starting point, turn on the system and note the location of sprinklers and/or drip emitters. If you know the start point, end point, and few points in between, you can figure out where the pipes are located.

- Evaluate the spray pattern of sprinklers. Turn on the system and note the spray patterns of sprinklers, including micro-sprinklers. Consider this, along with the mature height and width of the plant, when deciding on plant location. The spray pattern on some sprinklers may be adjustable. For example, a sprinkler that throws water in all directions can be adjusted to just cover part of the circle. Irrigation heads can be moved and you can also add risers to the pipe and spray over the plants.

- For sprinkler systems, estimate the delivery rate and application uniformity. Set out collection containers in a grid over the area and run the system for a set time. Then, measure the inches of water in each container and determine the average inches of water applied. Divide by the time the system ran. This is the application rate. The application uniformity can be assessed by comparing the inches of water in each container and by looking for muddy or dry spots.

- For drip (trickle) or micro-sprinkler/sprayer systems, inspect the emitters to assure they are delivering water. Emitters are usually above ground and can be damaged by crushing or wild life. Visually assess the application uniformity.

STEP 3 Sun and Shade

WHY IS THIS IMPORTANT?

Plants need sunlight to grow. They use it for photosynthesis, an important biological process that takes place in their leaves. In this process, plants make their own food from sunlight (the energy source) and raw materials from the soil and air (water and carbon dioxide). However, not all plants are created equal. Some need sun throughout the day during the growing season. Others manage with only morning or afternoon sun while some can tolerate shade for longer periods. Knowing where the sunny parts on your property are, where the sun comes in, and where it casts a shadow, will help choose the right plants for those areas. In an urban community garden located between two buildings, sun and shade issues are often critical.

ACTIVITIES

1. Patterns of light and shade

MATERIALS

- Camera
- Computer or other digital storage device
- Site assessment notebook

ESTIMATED TIME: 20 minutes for each time of the day.
Total: about 1 hour

This activity works well on sunny days. For areas that you are studying, take photos at three different times in a day—mid-morning, noon, and mid-afternoon—to discover sun and shade patterns. Mark the spot where you are standing, to make it easier to photograph from the same spot later.

Take photos from different angles, keeping a permanent feature in the photos (such as a fence, a patio, a part of the house, the street, etc.). *Don't use zoom.* Check your photos to be sure they will be recognizable and clearly show a permanent feature as a reference. Store photos on your computer or other digital storage device for easy access. It won't be necessary to make prints from the photos but you can if you prefer. Be sure to label the photos with the location, date, and time of day.

Pete photographs light and shade patterns in his garden.

Light and shade patterns vary during the day and are easiest to track as shadows pass over an open lawn area.

13

Repeat this step's activities during another time of year when light angles will be different. Use the same time of day from the initial photos for each of the three times. Record observations in your notebook.

2. Sun exposure

MATERIALS
○ Sketch from Step 1
○ Pencil
○ Compass (optional)

ESTIMATED TIME: 5 minutes

Determine where north, south, east, and west is on your property. The sun rises in the east and sets in the west. The direction clockwise from the east is south and clockwise from the west is north. You can use a compass to determine direction. Record North, South, East, and West on the sketch you created in Step 1.

Full sun is generally considered at least 6 hours of direct sunlight and is necessary for many plants, especially those that bear fruit. When designing a landscape or garden, remember that areas with southern exposure get the most sunlight. Partial sun or partial shade is 3–6 hours of sun each day. Shade is less than 3 hours of direct sunlight each

day, with filtered or dappled sun during the rest of the day. If a plant prefers some degree of shade, it can wilt or show signs of leaf scorch, such as brown edges, if it gets too much sun.

Shade can be created by buildings, trees, fences, walls, or hills. The northern side of a building, for

Fruiting crops like tomato and squash need at least six hours of sunlight while leafy vegetables like spinach and lettuce may tolerate less.

instance, is in the shade almost all day. The eastern side gets sun in the morning and the western side gets sun in the afternoon. For buildings, sunlight on the south side is considered full sun. In areas without buildings, full sun happens where there are no obstructions to sunlight.

You can create shade by planting a tree or building a structure. What is in full sun today could be in partial shade if you do something to change the exposure. Be especially careful to keep sun-loving gardens, such as vegetable or fruit gardens, away from trees. Trees can block sunlight and compete with crops for water and nutrients. On the other hand, if a tree or shrub is removed by a storm or intentionally, there will be a sunny spot that didn't exist before.

Tree fruits like these peaches should receive eight or more hours of sunlight each day.

Using What You Found in this Step

Where light is obstructed by walls, buildings, or other objects, plant shade-tolerant flowering annuals and perennials.

Your photos are a record of the light and shade patterns on your property and will be useful during the planning process. Lawns as well as vegetable, fruit, and other sun-loving gardens prefer 6 hours of sun per day. There are lawn grasses such as fescues for shadier areas, but most lawn grass types thrive in sunny locations; shade-tolerant ground covers may be used in areas as an alternative to lawn. Culinary herb gardens do best with 6 hours of sun per day, but can be productive with less sun.

To learn which flowering, shrub, tree, or ornamental plants prefer sun, shade, or partial sun/shade, refer to reference books, plant labels, nursery experts, or lists from Cooperative Extension offices and websites. It is generally advised to compare plant labels with book or website references for plant light-exposure preferences.

Winter sun can cause damage to broad-leaved evergreens, such as rhododendron and cherry laurel, even if they are hardy in your area. The southwestern exposure is the most damaging, as temperatures drop quickly when the sun goes down, resulting in a burn-like damage. Bark on young trees planted with a south or southwest exposure is prone to cracking in winter. Broad-leaved evergreens do well on evenly lighted sites, such as a site with northern exposure.

Plants Mentioned in Step 3

The common name is followed by the scientific name and then additional information if needed.

Cherry laurel – *Prunus laurocerasus*

Fescues – *Festuca* sp. – a genus of grass plants of about 300 species. In lawns, varieties of tall fescues, fine fescues, chewing fescues, hard fescues and creeping red fescues are used in shaded areas.

Peach – *Prunus persica*

Rhododendron – *Rhododendron* sp. – a genus of more than 900 species, which includes plants with the common names of azalea and rhododendron. When used as a common name, rhododendron refers to shrubs with large clusters of flowers.

For Further Reading

Sun gardening information is considered the norm in gardening. The following books specialize in a more challenging light situation—the shade garden.

Planting the Dry Shade Garden: The Best Plants for the Toughest Spot in Your Garden, by Graham Rice, Timber Press, Portland, Oregon, 2011.

Shade Gardening—The Time-Life Complete Gardener, Time-Life Education, New York, 1995.

Shade Gardening, edited by Ken Burke, Ortho Books, San Ramon, California, 1990.

The Complete Shade Gardener, by George Schenk, Timber Press, Portland, Oregon, 1991.

Hardiness and Microclimates

WHY IS THIS IMPORTANT?

Plants are capable of withstanding cold up to a point. Built into their genes is information on the temperatures they can tolerate. If temperatures drop below the tolerance level for a plant, the cold or ice crystals that form actually rupture cells in leaves, stems, or roots. Sometimes cold damage is temporary, due to unseasonably cold weather, and the plant recovers.

The term hardiness in gardening refers to a plant's tolerance to cold, not toughness or ability to endure. Hardiness zones are defined on the USDA Plant Hardiness Zone Map on the next page. The map is divided into 5°F zones and reports the average-annual minimum temperature, not the lowest temperature that has or will occur. The information is used by gardeners to determine which perennial plants are likely to survive through the winter.

Microclimates are areas where the climate is different from the surrounding areas. For example, areas within your boundaries that are colder or warmer, or may experience higher wind speeds or receive less rain, than the rest of your property. Microclimates can also refer to a band several miles long that includes your property. For example, large bodies of water that moderate temperatures or valleys that are prone to frost. Considering microclimates in your garden and landscape design will help you understand how the hardiness zone and frost dates may vary.

Many vegetable and other annual plants are cold-sensitive at the beginning and end of a growing season. The first and last frost dates define the growing season for most of them. See the sidebar on page 20. Some, like lettuce, peas, radish, spinach, kale, and cabbage are less cold-sensitive.

ACTIVITIES

1. How cold does it get?

MATERIALS

- Internet access
- Sketch from Step 1
- Site assessment notebook

ESTIMATED TIME: 15 minutes

Access USDA hardiness zone information from **http://planthardiness.ars.usda.gov/PHZMWeb/**

Your local library may provide internet access if you do not have access. In the upper-left corner of the page, type in your zip code. Click on "Find" and your hardiness zone will appear under the zip code. For example, type in 13811, and find that the hardiness zone is Zone 5b: -15° to -10°F. This means that the average-annual-minimum temperature is between -15° and -10°F.

You can also access a map that shows how the hardiness zone varies within your zip code. Starting

Pete checks the hardiness zone of his newly acquired property on the USDA web site.

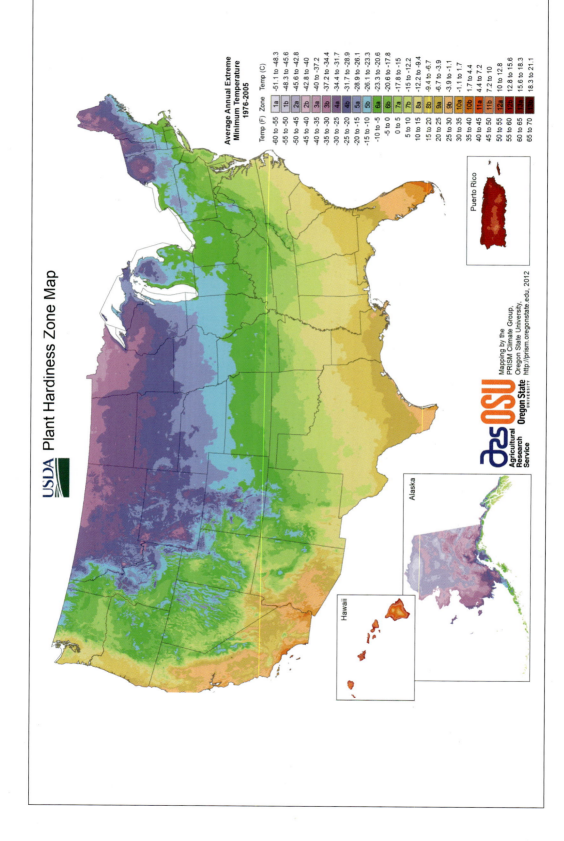

USDA Plant Hardiness Zone Map

Average Annual Extreme Minimum Temperature 1976-2005

Temp (F)	Zone	Temp (C)
-60 to -55	1a	-51.1 to -48.3
-55 to -50	1b	-48.3 to -45.6
-50 to -45	2a	-45.6 to -42.8
-45 to -40	2b	-42.8 to -40
-40 to -35	3a	-40 to -37.2
-35 to -30	3b	-37.2 to -34.4
-30 to -25	4a	-34.4 to -31.7
-25 to -20	4b	-31.7 to -28.9
-20 to -15	5a	-28.9 to -26.1
-15 to -10	5b	-26.1 to -23.3
-10 to -5	6a	-23.3 to -20.6
-5 to 0	6b	-20.6 to -17.8
0 to 5	7a	-17.8 to -15
5 to 10	7b	-15 to -12.2
10 to 15	8a	-12.2 to -9.4
15 to 20	8b	-9.4 to -6.7
20 to 25	9a	-6.7 to -3.9
25 to 30	9b	-3.9 to -1.1
30 to 35	10a	-1.1 to 1.7
35 to 40	10b	1.7 to 4.4
40 to 45	11a	4.4 to 7.2
45 to 50	11b	7.2 to 10
50 to 55	12a	10 to 12.8
55 to 60	12b	12.8 to 15.6
60 to 65	13a	15.6 to 18.3
65 to 70	13b	18.3 to 21.1

Puerto Rico

Hawaii

Alaska

OSU
Oregon State University

Agricultural Research Service

Mapping by the
PRISM Climate Group,
Oregon State University,
http://prism.oregonstate.edu, 2012

STEP 4: HARDINESS AND MICROCLIMATES

from the website above, click on "Interactive Map" in the top ribbon. In the upper-left corner of the page, type in your zip code. A map of the zip code area will appear showing the variation in hardiness zones. For zip code 13811, the hardiness zone will vary from 4b: -25° to -20°F to 6a: -10° to -5°F.

On your sketch, record the hardiness zone number and the average-annual-minimum temperature range. If you are near or on the border of another hardiness zone, note it in your notebook and consider it when selecting plants.

2. Microclimates

MATERIAL

○ Sketch started in Step 1

ESTIMATED TIME: 20 minutes

This activity focuses primarily on temperature microclimates within your property. Most properties will have areas that are colder or warmer than the rest of the property. Consider these microclimates when selecting plants. For example, if an area is colder than the rest of the property, you may want to choose plants with a hardiness rating lower than found in the previous activity. Microclimatic factors include:

□ **Reflected heat load** (heat pockets due to reflected heat from pavement, automobiles, buildings, or other surfaces.) This can cause trees and shrubs to heat up and lose water from their leaves at a faster-than-normal rate. These areas often face south and retain a tremendous amount of heat. On sunny days, these areas will be noticeably warmer than nearby spots. Temperatures along a south-facing wall will always be warmer; along a north-facing wall, cooler.

□ **Frost pockets** (often found in low areas at the bottom of a slope or bowl) are areas where cooler, heavier air can collect.

Plants in an urban environment can be stressed by heat reflected from hot pavements and buildings.

Bowls formed by surrounding hills may be prone to frost pockets.

□ **Moderation of climate** (fewer extremes of temperature) may occur when a site is located near a large body of water.

□ **Rain shadows** (areas sheltered from natural rainfall except as occasionally blown in by the wind) An overhang from a porch or higher roof can block rain from falling beneath it creating a rain shadow. Gardens or containerized plants under a rain shadow will need to be watered. Rain shadows can also form on the rainless side of a solid fence or wall. Trees can also prevent rain from reaching the ground and their roots will draw water and nutrients in large quantities.

garden. Make sure the types and cultivars of the plants you choose are expected to fare well over winter in your area. Hardiness zones are general guidelines only. For example, the amount of snow or rain during a year is also a factor. Cultivars of a particular species can have different hardiness.

Staff and Master Gardeners in county Cooperative Extension offices are good advisors on local hardiness observations.

Hardiness won't be very important in choosing annual flowers, annual vegetables, or annual herbs; they only live one season, dying before winter arrives. For them, the last spring frost date is needed for planning planting dates.

Consider the microclimates on or encompassing your property as you select plants and design gardens and landscapes. Spots may be colder or warmer than the hardiness zone suggests. Choose plants from a slightly colder hardiness zone in frost pockets. A maximum-minimum thermometer is useful for evaluating low temperatures in frost pockets or high temperatures where there is reflected heat. It shows the maximum and minimum temperature since it was last set.

Choose drought-resistant trees for sites where there are reflected heat loads. Consider reflected heat load for shrubs and herbaceous plants as well. Shrubs or herbaceous plants in these areas may need more frequent watering.

■ **Wind** hitting the side of house, solid fence, or wall, creates turbulence and higher wind speeds along the surface and its edge or corner. In Step 5, wind and its effects are discussed in more depth.

On the property sketch started in Step 1, indicate the location of any reflected heat load spots, frost pockets, and rain shadows. Indicate reflected heat load areas on your sketch only if they appear to be an ongoing, persistent concern.

USING WHAT YOU FOUND IN THIS STEP

Plants are categorized by their hardiness zones. As you read through the catalogs or purchase plants in garden centers or online, eliminate any plant that has a hardiness zone rating with a number higher than your zone. For instance, if you live in Zone 5 (*a* or *b*), plants that are rated as hardy to Zone 2, 3, 4, or 5 will overwinter. The *a* and *b* designations for plants are not always available. Plants that have a hardiness rating of Zone 6 or higher may not make it through the winter. Plants can also be listed as hardy in a range of zones. Some plant selection databases can sort plants by hardiness zone.

Use hardiness information when you are selecting plants for your fruit, landscape, or perennial

Lakes moderate temperatures resulting in fewer extremes.

Shrubs in the rain shadow (under the overhang) struggle while adjacent plants thrive.

Avoid planting vegetable gardens in low-lying frost pockets. They will be more productive if they get an early start in the spring, grow under normal temperatures, and grow longer into the fall. In the spring, fruit-tree flowers are especially vulnerable to late frosts. When fruit-tree flowers are killed by frost, they will not produce fruit.

Where rain shadows exist, consider mulching with stone pebbles under the overhang. Plants are best positioned in front of a rain shadow. If you plant in a rain shadow, plan on watering plants by hand or hose regularly.

If your property experiences high winds, plantings along a wall may be subject to drying winds. Consider this when selecting plants for the area.

What are Frost Dates?

When plans include annual plants, the last spring frost date helps you determine when to plant. The first fall frost dates are important if you are estimating how long your annuals will be in bloom or how long your vegetables can be harvested. Annual plants are those that complete their life cycle in one growing season and have to be replanted each year. This includes vegetables, some herbs, and annual flowers.

To determine the first and last frost you will need to access this website: **http://www.almanac.com/content/frost-chart-united-states**

Scroll down this page to find a list of cities with their frost dates and growing season length. If your location is not near one of these cities, scroll to the bottom of the list and find a place to click for more information. This will bring you to a page where you can download PDF files of frost dates for your state. Find the location nearest to yours and use those frost dates.

For each location, there are three dates given for three different temperature thresholds depending on the probability of occurrence. For example, three dates are reported for each of three temperatures. For a threshold temperature of 32°F in Addison NY, April 30, May 18, and June 4 are given. It tells you that there

is a 90% chance that the last frost will not occur until April 30, a 50% chance the last frost will not occur until May 18, and a 10% chance that the last frost will not occur until June 4. There is a 90% chance that the last 28°F temperature will not occur until April 17, and a 90% chance that the last 36°F temperature will not occur until May 7. Pick a temperature and record the dates for the last spring and first fall frost dates at each probability level. Record this information in your site assessment notebook.

As you zero in on the annuals (vegetable, herb or flower) to be planted for the next season, decide whether you want to be conservative and wait until the last possible spring frost date to plant or get a head start on a few, like peas or lettuce, at the earlier end of the last spring frost date. Raised beds and terraces will warm earlier in the spring, especially south-facing ones. The first fall frost dates are important if you are estimating how long your annuals will be in bloom or how long your vegetables can be harvested. For instance, the herb basil is one of the first plants to go after the first fall frost.

Your local Cooperative Extension office or university-based state gardening program may also be able to tell you frost dates for your area.

Plants Mentioned in Step 4

The common name is followed by the scientific name.

Basil – *Ocimum basilicum*
Lettuce – *Lactuca sativa*
Peas – *Pisum sativum*

For Further Reading

Visit **http://www.hort.cornell.edu/site/** *for links to the web sites below and all web sites mentioned in this book.*

Frost

http://www.almanac.com/content/frost-chart-united-states
From the Old Farmers Almanac

http://www.gardening.cornell.edu/weather/frost.pdf
From Cornell University

Microclimates

http://blogs.cornell.edu/horticulture/microclimate/
From Cornell University

USDA Plant Hardiness Zone Map

http://planthardiness.ars.usda.gov/PHZMWeb/
Hardiness zone designations for all parts of the United States. Detailed information for an area can be found by entering a zip code on the upper left of the web page or by using the interactive map. From the United States Department of Agriculture.

5 Wind

Plantings near bodies of water and on hill tops, balconies, terraces, and rooftops may experience frequent strong winds.

WHY IS THIS IMPORTANT?

Whether you are gardening in an open landscape or on a terrace in a high-rise apartment building, wind will affect the plants you are growing. Gentle breezes may be beneficial by allowing healthy air exchanges. Still air may promote disease organisms, while good air flow reduces their population. Stronger winds that blow occasionally before, during, or after a storm are inevitable in most locations. The microclimates created by winds have varying affects depending on the wind's intensity and frequency.

However, if your site is located where strong winds blow on a regular basis or during certain seasons of the year, pay special attention to the effect the winds have on your landscape. Locations near lakes or on hilltops are especially vulnerable to frequent winds. Balcony or terrace gardens on high-rise apartments may have a serious wind problem. Setting plants that are intolerant of wind on those sites is aesthetically and financially

disastrous. The plants are stressed and less able to sustain good health.

Winds can dry out a plant quicker than the roots can draw up replacement water. Water is a key component of every cell in the plant. Wind accelerates evaporation from leaf surfaces, causing plants to undergo stress. Some plants are able to withstand wind better than others, and may be planted as windbreaks. Other plants are quite sensitive to the drying effect, or desiccation, caused by wind.

Plants, including trees, are most vulnerable when they are first planted or transplanted. Roots are not established and the plant has not adjusted to its new environment. On windy sites, plants can die during the first or second year after planting. In the winter, when the ground is frozen or dry, wind can do the most damage. Winter wind can damage trees or shrubs.

Wind damage may show up on wind-intolerant broad-leaved evergreens (like holly, cherry laurel, and rhododendron). While damaged leaves can be pruned out, it is not advisable to plant these evergreens in sites where they will be wind damaged annually.

ACTIVITY

Where are my windy spots?

MATERIALS
- 10 or more sticks longer than 2 feet
- Roll of flagging tape or ribbon
- Wristwatch or stopwatch
- Camera
- Sketch started in Step 1
- Site assessment notebook

ESTIMATED TIME: 1 hour to set up (one time only) and 1 minute to record each site. Total time varies with the number of sites you choose, but it will be 1.5 to 2 hours.

This activity will require setup and periodic monitoring. It will be done over a longer time than activities in other steps. Do this activity during different seasons, including winter, to get a complete picture of wind patterns. This activity is a good family project or an organized youth group project in a community garden.

Sites surrounded by fences, woodland, or mature plantings that protect from or buffer wind are less likely to suffer wind damage. This activity is optional for sites with wind buffers.

Collect 10 or more sticks or old twigs and tie about a foot of flagging tape to each. Choose sticks that are about the same length and at least two feet high. Use non-adhesive and lightweight flagging tape so it moves freely with the wind. It will dangle during still, windless times.

Select at least ten sites on your property that are out in the open and insert the flag into the ground securely. Number each site.

In your notebook make a chart with dates to record observations (every few days or weekly will be sufficient). Randomly

Herb is puzzled by the flagging tape.

choose morning, afternoon, and evening times on different dates. Allow space to record the stick number and the status of the flag for a one-minute interval. Do this for several days over a month, if possible. Observe and record at the times you designate. The chart for one day might look something like this, but use your discretion.

Observe and record the estimated angle between the stick and the flagging tape. On a still day, the angle is 0 degrees. On a very windy day, the angle is 90 degrees or more. With a stopwatch or wristwatch, record how long the tape stays at each site at that angle over a one-minute interval. Indicate if the flag is still or moving frequently.

Indicate on your sketch from Step 1 if there are particularly windy spots on your property. You do not have to mark every location you tested, only those that may be a problem.

Date	Time of day	Location	Angle of flag in estimated degrees	% of one-minute interval (with movement)
2/10	10 am	1	0	0 (no wind)
		2	0	0 (no wind)
		3	15	10 (fairly still)
		4	45	50 (moves frequently)
		5	90	50 (fairly windy)

This activity consumes more time than others in this work book. Doing it over a month's time and at random intervals may show a trend or pattern. Don't run out only if the day is windy, nor confine your observations to days when there is no breeze. Hopefully, random observations will yield results that are typical of the property's wind exposure. This is not scientific evidence, but a record for the study time chosen.

Using What You Found in this Step

There is not a formula for assessing what you have observed. You will end up making a judgment call on whether you have a very windy site or just a few spots where the wind potentially could be a problem. Take a photo showing the location of the sticks and flags and keep this with the chart. The photo will help you remember where the sticks were located after they are removed.

On windy sites, choose wind-tolerant plants such as junipers, Eastern redbud, common hackberry, flowering quince, bayberry, mugo pine, and white oak. Avoid plants that do not tolerate strong winds such as Japanese maple, boxwood, wisteria, evergreen hollies, yews, Eastern arborvitae, and flowering dogwood.

Anti-desiccants are effective in protecting broad-leaved evergreens from excessive wind damage in winter. Anti-desiccants are clear films sprayed on the leaves of plants to seal the invisible

Burlap wrap on evergreens provides protection from desiccating winter winds.

pores and prevent excessive water loss; they last for a few months. They are often used on newly planted broad-leaved evergreens over the winter. Burlap, wrapped around a newly planted evergreen in winter, can also provide protection from desiccating winds. However, if you find it necessary to use anti-desiccants or burlap wrapping on the same plant every year, consider relocating the plant.

For severely windy sites, windbreaks may be necessary. Windbreaks are rows of wind-tolerant trees or shrubs, such as Eastern white pine, that reduce or redirect the wind, creating stiller air on the protected side. Tree height and density, windbreak orientation, and other factors are considered when siting a windbreak.

Fruit, vegetable, or other herbaceous plant gardens are best located where there are gentle breezes, not strong wind. Good air circulation helps prevent disease.

Sometimes neighbors' experiences with similar exposure to winds on their property are helpful. Each property's wind patterns vary, but there may be commonalities for you to consider.

Plants Mentioned in Step 5

The common name is followed by the scientific name and then additional information if needed.

Bayberry – *Myrica* sp. – a genus of more than 30 species, sometimes called myrtle. Usually *Myrica pensylvanica* is the common bayberry.

Boxwood – *Buxus* sp. – a genus of over 70 species; the most common is *Buxus sempervirens*.

Cherry laurel – *Prunus laurocerasus*

Common hackberry – *Celtis occidentalis*

Eastern arborvitae – *Thuja occidentalis* – also called American arborvitae.

Eastern redbud – *Cercis canadensis*

Eastern white pine – *Pinus strobus*

Flowering dogwood – *Cornus florida*

Flowering quince – *Chaenomeles japonica, C. speciosa*, or one of their hybrids,

Holly – *Ilex* sp. – a genus of over 500 species, most of which are evergreen.

Japanese maple – *Acer palmatum* – a species of over a thousand cultivars.

Juniper – *Juniperus* sp. – a genus of over fifty species.

Mugo pine – *Pinus mugo*

Rhododendron – *Rhododendron* sp. – a genus of more than 900 species, which includes plants with the common names of azalea and rhododendron. When used as a common name, rhododendron refers to shrubs with large clusters of flowers. While *Rhododendron* sp. can be either evergreen or deciduous, the most commonly planted rhododendrons are evergreen.

White oak – *Quercus alba*

Wisteria – *Wisteria* sp. – a genus of about 8 species; the most common are *Wisteria sinensis* (Chinese wisteria), *Wisteria floribunda* (Japanese wisteria), and *Wisteria frutescens* (American wisteria).

Yew – *Taxus* sp. – a genus of about 9 species; the most common are Taxus baccata (common yew) and Taxus cuspidata (Japanese yew).

For Further Reading

The Exuberant Garden and the Controlling Hand, by William H. Frederick, Jr. Little Brown and Co., New York, 1992. See appendix A "Summary of Cultural Preferences and Tolerances."

Landscape Plants for Eastern North America, 2nd edition, by Harrison L. Flint, John Wiley and Sons, Inc., Hoboken, New Jersey, 1997. Shows wind tolerance for many landscape trees, shrubs, and vines. A useful reference for landscape professionals, but not easily accessible for home gardeners.

Visit **http://www.hort.cornell.edu/site/** *for a link to the web site below and all web sites mentioned in this book.*

<u>Windbreaks</u>

http://extension.psu.edu/plants/plasticulture/ production-details/windbreaks

Information on height, density, orientation, and other factors affecting a windbreak. From Penn State University.

25

Compaction

Why Is This Important?

Soil is made up of mineral particles—sand, silt, and clay. But it also has essential spaces between the particles, some small and some larger. While these pore spaces are usually tiny to the naked eye, the larger pores provide space for both water and air. They also allow excess water to drain out, creating an air space, and preventing the roots of plants from becoming waterlogged. A compacted soil has little to none of these larger pores. The large pores are crushed. The smaller pores are suited to hold water, but do not allow the excess to drain off. The pores are completely filled with water, with no room left for oxygen. This inhibits root formation and overall plant growth. Plants can not grow in compacted soil.

Compaction happens when heavy machinery, vehicles, or foot traffic compresses or packs down the soil reducing the pore size and pore space. With new construction, it is likely that the soil has been compacted by construction equipment. Compaction is often an issue in community gardens located where a building was demolished or where there has been construction activity.

source: Ken Sherman

Test for compaction and heavy metals when community gardens will be located where a building was demolished.

Heavy vehicles are one cause of soil compaction. Eventually the tracks will disappear, but the soil will still be compacted.

ACTIVITIES

1. Are there spots with compacted soil?

MATERIALS

- Long-handled, pointed-blade shovel
- Clipboard (or flat, hard-surfaced item)
- Paper and pencil
- Masking tape
- Waterproof marker
- 10–25 sticks (wooden skewer sticks, for instance)
- A friend, neighbor, or family member (as a reality check)
- Sketch started in Step 1
- Site assessment notebook

ESTIMATED TIME: 15 minutes of preparation and 15 minutes per person for 10 test spots

This activity is allied to the activities on drainage (infiltration and percolation) in Step 7. In this step however, the focus is on the physical nature of the soil and how easy or difficult it is to dig. It is an activity involving some guesswork and judgment rather than a specific measurement. We use such phrases as "it feels like" or "it seems that." Do this test when the soil is relatively dry, when it hasn't rained for several days.

Walk around 10 or more areas of the property. Mark spots you will test with the sticks. Use paper to make flag-like markers and tape them to the stick. Mark each with a unique number. Choose spots at random, or mark areas where you suspect you will be putting a

Pete checks for soil compaction.

landscape, vegetable garden, flower bed, shade tree, or lawn. Don't worry if you aren't sure where those elements will be located. You can always do a follow-up test later. For now, just get an idea of how compact your soil is in different parts of the property.

Use your foot to push the point of a long-handled shovel about halfway into the ground. If the shovel hits a stone, move it a little to get a true test. For especially stoney sites, a rebar works well. If you hit thick tree roots, repeat the test nearby to determine the extent of the roots. If tree roots are extensive, stop testing that area for compaction.

Compare how much effort you used in each area, and rate each spot as *hard*, *average*, or *easy*. Keep track of your findings in your notebook. Since your ratings are based on what it feels like to you, ask someone else to do the push test and compare results.

Everyone's strength will be different on this test, but after a few trials, you will get the sense of it. Each *hard*, *average*, and *easy* rating is relative to the other areas of your property. While this test is far from precise, it helps in locating problem areas. It is not uncommon for gardeners to discover areas with compacted soil on their sites.

2. Visual Observations

MATERIALS

- Site assessment notebook

ESTIMATED TIME: 5 minutes

- Has the area been used for frequent parties? Are there footpaths that people have created?
- Is the area sometimes used for parking?
- Is this a new home site? Was there an addition added? Construction equipment may have compacted soil.

Record relevant information in your notebook.

USING WHAT YOU FOUND IN THIS STEP

Mark on your property sketch areas that may be potential problems. Use letter codes on the sketch and add the codes to the sketch's legend. Use simple codes such as:

- *C* for compact (*hard* ratings)
- *PC* for partially compact (*average* ratings)
- *TR* for excessive tree roots

C spots need priority attention if they will be used for plants. There is always room for soil improvement on the *PC* spots. It isn't necessary to mark the spots where the shovel was easy to push through the soil (*easy* ratings). Avoid planting where there are tree roots close to the soil surface.

Amending compacted soil with organic matter will help loosen the soil and re-establish larger pore spaces. Add at least 25% organic matter for a sandy soil and 50% organic matter for a clayey soil. For example, a 10-foot by 10-foot area is 100 square feet. If you dig down 1 foot, the total volume is 100 cubic feet. 50% of 100 cubic feet is 50 cubic feet. So, mix in 50 cubic feet, almost 2 cubic yards, of organic matter in the 100 cubic feet of clayey soil.

Try to amend an entire bed, not just a planting hole. As roots grow, they move into the surrounding soil, so it helps to have an uncompacted area instead of just an uncompacted planting spot. The amount of organic matter needed depends on site characteristics.

On a compacted site slated to become a vegetable garden, plant cover crops the year before your first planting. To avoid future compaction in vegetable gardens, use wide beds with permanent paths or board planks to walk on between planting. Gardens that require frequent and regular weeding and harvesting are prone to compaction by human feet.

In very compacted soil, you might need a special tool called a mattock or pickax to break through the soil before amending it.

For areas with compacted soil or frequent foot or car traffic, consider hardscaping. Hardscaping replaces the grass or compacted soil with stone, brick, paving, or other non-plant material.

Using a pickax to break up compacted soil on a former parking lot site.

Foot traffic was significant enough to install a more durable path. This paved path in the same location will be maintenance-free for years.

For Further Reading

Visit http://www.hort.cornell.edu/site/ for links to the web sites below and all web sites mentioned in this book.

Dealing with Soil Compaction

www.gardening.cornell.edu/factsheets/soil/compaction.html

By Nina Bassuk, Urban Horticulture Institute, Cornell University

Improve Your Soil with Cover Crops

http://blogs.cornell.edu/horticulture/about/basic-gardening-info/cover-crops/

From Cornell Garden Based Learning, Department of Horticulture, Cornell University.

Using Organic Matter in the Garden

www.gardening.cornell.edu/factsheets/orgmatter/index.html

Information on how much organic matter to add to different kinds of garden and landscape sites. From Cornell Cooperative Extension by Charles Mazza, Sally Cunningham, and Ellen Harrison.

Drainage

WHY IS THIS IMPORTANT?

Many gardens and landscapes have been devastated by poor drainage. Areas on your property that puddle after a rain or are continuously wet indicate a condition that is stressful for most plants.

The vast majority of our garden and landscape plants have root systems that can only thrive where the soil provides both air and water. If the essential, vast network of pore spaces in the soil is filled with water, air is forced out, robbing roots of oxygen. Some plants may languish for months or years, while others succumb quickly. A well-drained soil has water in it, but no puddles.

On the other hand, it is possible to create a landscape or garden on a site where the water drains slowly. There are a small number of plants that can tolerate and even thrive in wet or poorly drained sites. Using them is an option for soils with poor drainage.

There are two ways to learn how your soil drains. One is to measure the infiltration rate, how rapidly water moves into the surface of soil. It is especially useful for lawn areas or gardens where shallow rooted plants, such as annuals or most herbaceous perennials, will grow. The other is to measure the percolation rate, how rapidly water drains out—deep down in the soil. Knowing the percolation rate helps in planning landscapes with trees and shrubs, where the roots push deeper into the soil.

Saucer magnolias flower best on well-drained sites. The one on the left is on a well-drained site, the one on the right is on a site that floods periodically. The photos were taken on the same day about a mile apart.

ACTIVITIES

1. Infiltration test (adapted from interview with Dr. Tammo Steenhuis, Department of Biological and Environmental Engineering, Cornell University)

MATERIALS

- Empty 11- to 16-oz. coffee can or other can with a diameter of 3 inches or more.
- Can opener
- Ruler
- Waterproof marker
- 2 cups of water
- Kitchen timer
- Wooden board, 1–2 ft. long (optional)
- Site assessment notebook

ESTIMATED TIME: for each test location – 5 minutes to set up and up to 1 hour of waiting and observing time

Pete times how long it takes for water to soak down during an infiltration test.

Do this test when the soil is relatively wet. Wait for a few hours after a soaking rain or wet the area with a hose and wait for an hour or so.

- Remove the top and bottom of the empty can.
- Countersink the can into the soil, so that approximately ⅓ of the can is sticking up above the soil. Use a board to help push it in, if necessary. Measure and mark, with a waterproof marker, two lines on the inside—one at a 1-inch point and the other at a 2-inch point above the soil surface. This can be done on a grassy site, but it might be easier to measure if you did it on a bare soil surface. If the soil surface has a crusty look, make a note in the space provided; it may affect how water penetrates.

- Fill the can with water to the 2" line. That's about two cups of water. Set the timer for one hour.

- In your notebook, record the time it takes for the water to soak down (infiltrate). Record the level two or three times during the first half-hour and then every five minutes in the last half-hour. If, at the end of one hour, water remains in the can, measure and record how far down the water has dropped. Calculate the infiltration rate by dividing the distance the water level moved by the time it took. Convert all measurements to inches per hour. For instance, if water moved 1.5 inches in 0.5 hours, that is 3 inches per hour.

Rate your soil for surface infiltration.

Inches per hour	Surface Drainage
less than 0.4	poor
0.4–2	moderate
2–8	good
greater than 8	excessive

- Record your results in your site assessment notebook.

- Do the test where new plantings are being considered especially if the area was identified as compacted in Step 6, is frequently wet, or puddles after rain.

2. Percolation test (adapted from *Trees and the Urban Landscape; Site Assessment, Design, and Installation*, 2004, by P.J. Trowbridge and N.L. Bassuk, pp. 32, 35. John Wiley & Sons, Hoboken, NJ.)

MATERIALS

- Shovel
- Plastic sheet or large bucket for soil
- Yardstick
- Water
- Kitchen timer
- Site assessment notebook

ESTIMATED TIME: for each test location – 15 minutes to set up and observe and 1–2 hours of waiting time

- Dig a hole about 1 to 1.5 feet wide and deep removing the soil and storing it on a plastic sheet or in a bucket. If the test location is in a lawn, remove about 1 sq. ft. of sod before digging.

- Fill the hole with water two or three times to saturate the soil lining the hole. Thoroughly plan, you can do this activity for additional sites later. If your planting plan is uncertain, test a site that might have questionable drainage to determine if it is a limitation.

☐ Dig a hole 12–15 inches deep, removing several clods of soil for examination as you dig. Clods that look grayish (with or without reddish markings) or have a rotting-vegetation and/or rotten-egg smell indicate that the site has poor drainage. Replace the clods after observations are complete.

☐ Record the observations in your notebook.

3b. Visual Observations
Topography

MATERIALS

○ Site assessment notebook

ESTIMATED TIME: 5–10 minutes

Study the topography, or lay of the land, for low-lying areas that may collect surface runoff and may be poorly drained. Observe these areas immediately after a heavy rain. Record the observations in your notebook.

Inches per hour	Drainage
less than 4	poor
4–8	moderate
greater than 8	excessive

☐ Check your results on another spot, or more, for reassurance.

☐ Record the results in your notebook.

☐ Do the test where new plantings are being considered especially if the area is compacted, frequently wet, or puddles after rain. A percolation test is especially important for proposed tree or shrub locations.

3a. Visual Observations
Examine Sub Soil

MATERIALS

○ Long-handled, pointed-blade shovel
○ Site assessment notebook

ESTIMATED TIME: 10 minutes for each hole

☐ Choose a site where you want to place a major tree, shrub, or vine, or develop an entire garden of edibles or ornamentals. If you change the

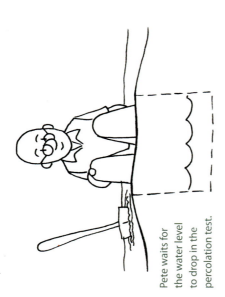

Pete waits for the water level to drop in the percolation test.

wet an area about 1 foot around the hole. Let the water drain completely before starting the percolation test.

☐ Fill the thoroughly saturated hole with water and immediately measure the depth of the water with a yardstick. Set a timer for 15 minutes.

☐ After 15 minutes, measure the water depth again. Record the difference in inches in your notebook. Multiply the result by 4. This gives you the percolation rate in inches per hour.

☐ Rate your soil's percolation rate.

3c. Visual Observations
Indicator Plants

MATERIALS

○ Site assessment notebook

ESTIMATED TIME: Ongoing observations

Look for trees (indicator plants) that suggest soil drainage conditions. Trees indicating poorly drained (wet) sites include willow, swamp white oak, and tupelo. Trees indicating moist soils are sycamores and tulip trees. Trees indicating well-drained sites are sugar maple, red oak, and hickories. Record observations in your notebook. In Step 11, you will include the trees in a plant inventory.

USING WHAT YOU FOUND IN THIS STEP

When the infiltration is good and the percolation rate is moderate, you have good gardening conditions. If the infiltration rate is excessive consider installing a rain garden on a slightly sloping site at least 10 feet from your house. Plants in the rain garden are watered using rain water collected from the roof of your house.

If the infiltration rate is poor or moderate and the percolation rate is moderate, you may have compaction just below the surface. The plant roots of future gardens, combined with applying surface mulch and amending with organic matter, may alleviate the problem. A poor percolation rate indicates a poorly drained site and an excessive percolation rate indicates drought-prone sites—both challenging gardening conditions.

If there are small, poorly drained areas, indicate them on your sketch with a "W" for wet. Add the code to the sketch's legend. For larger areas, sketch their approximate size as well. When you design, select plants that are suitable for wet sites, such as turtlehead, elderberry, and deciduous holly. For lawn areas, liriope is a possible substitute for chronic, poorly drained areas that cannot be adequately amended. Fruit and vegetable plantings are best located on well-drained sites with no standing water after a rain.

Using plants that tolerate wet sites does not change the wetness; plants cannot absorb excessive water to make the site drier. Where sites are constantly wet, they may be part of a wetland area and wetland protection laws may apply. Contact your county's Soil and Water Conservation District (SWCD) for advice. One way to get contact information for your county's SWCD is to search the web using "SWCD–your county's name and state."

It is possible to correct sites with occasional puddling or poor drainage. Raising the entire bed, adding soil with better draining capabilities, amending the soil with organic matter, and installing drainage pipes are options. You may also choose not to garden in those spots.

When the percolation rate is excessive, the area will dry out

Underground pipes can shunt water away from an area where it collects.

frequently. On your sketch, indicate these areas with a "D" for dry. Add the code to the sketch's legend. Use drought-tolerant plants in these areas such as stonecrop, Eastern redbud, and shrubby cinquefoil.

PLANTS MENTIONED IN STEP 7

The common name is followed by the scientific name and then additional information if needed.

Deciduous holly – *Ilex verticillata* – also called winterberry, American winterberry, winterberry holly. *Ilex decidua* – also called possum haw or swamp holly.
Eastern redbud – *Cercis canadensis*

Elderberry is a good choice for poorly drained sites, even along ditches.

Elderberry – *Sambucus* sp. – a genus of about 12 species; the most common species is *Sambucus canadensis*. Also may be called elder.

Hickory – *Carya* sp. – a genus of about 18 species; the most common are *Carya ovata* (Shagbark hickory) and *Carya glabra* (Pignut hickory).

Liriope – a genus, but often used as a common name, along with lilyturf (although it is neither a lily nor a grass). *Liriope muscari* and *Liriope spicata* are two of the most common species used as ground covers.

Saucer magnolia – *Magnolia* × *soulaneana*

Shrubby cinquefoil – *Potentilla fruticosa* – a species with over 80 cultivars.

Stonecrop – *Sedum* sp. – a genus of over 400 species. Sedum is used as a common name as well. One of the most commonly used sedums in landscaping is one of the cultivars or hybrids of showy sedum, *Sedum spectabile*.

Sugar maple – *Acer saccharum*

Swamp white oak – *Quercus bicolor*

Sycamore – *Platanus* sp. – a genus of three or four species in North America. The most common is *Platanus occidentalis*. Often crossed with *Platanus orientalis* to form a hybrid widely planted in North America, *Plantanus* × *acerifolia* (London plane tree), sometimes referred to commonly as a sycamore. Also known as buttonwood in America or plane trees in Europe.

Tulip tree – *Liriodendron tulipifera*

Tupelo – *Nyssa* sp. – a genus of about 10 species; the most common is *Nyssa sylvatica*. Also known as black gum or pepperidge tree.

Turtlehead – *Chelone oblique* or *Chelone glabra*, herbaceous perennials.

Willow – *Salix* sp. – a genus of about 400 species of deciduous trees and shrubs.

FOR FURTHER READING

Tough Plants for Tough Places, by Gary Vergine and Michael Jefferson-Brown, Contemporary Books, Chicago, Illinois, 1997. Section 1 discusses plants for sites that are too dry. Section 2 discusses plants for sites that are too wet.

Visit http://www.hort.cornell.edu/site/ for a link to the web sites below and all web sites mentioned in this book.

<u>Drought Tolerant Plants</u>

www.backyardgardener.com/dry/
From the BackyardGardener.com.

<u>Rain Gardens</u>

http://learningstore.uwex.edu/pdf/GWQ037.pdf
Detailed homeowner instructions on creating a rain garden from the University of Wisconsin. Developed by Roger Bannerman, Wisconsin Department of Natural Resources and Ellen Considine, U.S. Geological Survey.

<u>Soil Drainage</u>

www.cmg.colostate.edu/gardennotes/219.pdf
Colorado Master Gardener Notes #219 by D. Whiting, A. Card, C. Wilson.

<u>Soil Moisture Chart for Trees and Shrubs</u>

www.hort.cornell.edu/uhi/outreach/recurbtree/pdfs/09soilh2oph.pdf
From *Recommended Urban Trees: Site Assessment and Tree Selection for Stress Tolerance*, Urban Horticulture Institute, Cornell University, 2009.

8 Soil Characteristics

WHY IS THIS IMPORTANT?

Soil can make or break a garden or landscape because it supplies water and nutrients to plants through the plants' roots. Too much or too little of either can hurt plant health. The physical and chemical composition of soil varies from place to place and can even be different within the same yard. Considering soil characteristics will help you select plants that will thrive.

The physical composition of soil is determined by the soil's texture—the relative amounts of sand, silt, and clay in the soil. Knowing the soil's physical composition will help you make informed decisions later in the process. The chemical composition of the soil—the levels of nutrients present and its pH—affects nutrient uptake by plants. For example, some plants (such as blueberries and rhododendrons) require acidic soil.

ACTIVITIES

1. What's the physical composition of my soil?—Soil Sedimentation Test

MATERIALS

- Pointed shovel
- Bucket
- Sealable plastic bag
- Pint-sized glass jar with tightly fitting lid—the narrower the better (an olive jar works well)
- Kitchen timer, watch, or electronic timer
- Powdered dishwasher detergent
- Ruler
- Masking tape
- Site assessment notebook

ESTIMATED TIME: 20 minutes of collecting, observing, and recording. Overnight for drying the soil. It may take 2–3 days to complete the test.

1. To get a good overview of soil characteristics, take soil from 10 locations around the study area. Dig holes 6 to 8 inches deep. Then take a vertical slice of soil from the edge and place it into the bucket. Mix them all together. Measure one cup of mixed soil for this first activity. Save another cup in a sealed plastic bag for the next activity on measuring the soil's pH.

2. Let the soil dry and remove stones, roots, grass, or other debris.

3. Apply a strip of masking tape vertically to the pint-sized glass jar. (Later you'll mark levels on the tape.)

4. Add one cup of dried, debris-free soil to the jar. Add water until the jar is about ⅔ to ¾ full.

5. Screw on the lid and shake well to put the soil into suspension.

6. Add one teaspoon of powdered dishwasher detergent. Shake again.

Pete does a soil sedimentation test indoors with Herb watching.

7. Place the jar on a flat surface where it can remain undisturbed for several days. Set the timer for one minute.

8. At the end of one minute, mark on the masking tape the level of soil particles that have settled to the bottom. This will be the sand component.

9. Reset the timer. At the end of 2 hours mark on the masking tape the level where the soil particles have settled to the bottom. This second layer is the silt component.

10. It may take several days for the clay component to settle out. Mark the level tentatively after two or three days. Check and mark daily after that. If the level doesn't rise from one day to the next, use that line as your final level. Even after several days, the water will remain cloudy as a small percentage of clay particles will remain in suspension.

11. The layers reflect the percentage of sand, silt, and clay in the soil. Divide the thickness of each layer by the total height of settled soil (not the height of the water, just the settled soil). Multiply by 100 to find the percentage of sand, silt, and clay. Record the percentage of sand, silt, and clay in your notebook.

12. Any darkly colored material floating in suspension in the water is organic matter. Estimate whether you have none, a little (negligible), or a substantial amount. Estimating organic matter

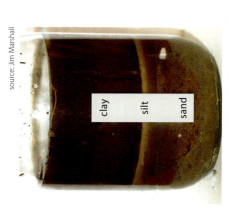

source: Jim Marshall

This soil is approximately 45% sand, 5% silt, and 50% clay. Organic matter is negligible.

is difficult because it has many more air pockets and is looser than the mineral soil sediment. Record observations in your notebook.

People with experience in different types of soils also estimate texture by manipulating it in their hand and feeling it.

2. What is the pH—acidity or alkalinity—of my soil?

MATERIALS

- Soil saved in sealable plastic bag from first activity
- Site assessment notebook

ESTIMATED TIME: Collecting time is included in the first activity; waiting time at lab will vary.

Use the soil collected during Activity 1 in this step. If the sample is wet, spread the soil in a thin layer on an aluminum pie pan, clean wrapping paper, or waxed paper, and allow it to dry out at room temperature. Remove stones, roots, and debris.

While home pH test kits are available from garden centers, many gardeners struggle to get accurate and consistent results. Contact your local Cooperative Extension office to see if they operate a lab that can test soil pH. If they can't, ask them for instructions to send your sample to a reputable soil lab.

Record the soil's pH in your notebook. pH may vary around the property. When you consider locations for plantings, test the location's pH.

3a. Visual Observations
Soil Appearance

MATERIALS:

- Long-handled, pointed shovel
- Site assessment notebook

ESTIMATED TIME: 30 minutes

In this activity, you will examine the soil horizons or layers. It is especially useful if there has been recent construction activity. If you are not aware of past construction activity, choose an undisturbed location at random to get a better idea of topsoil depth.

Dig a pit approximately two feet deep and two feet wide. Soil layers that are noticeably lighter in color than lower layers indicate that subsoil has been spread on top of the original soil. Conversely, the absence of a rich brown, organic layer at the top may indicate that the topsoil has been removed. In undisturbed soils, estimate the depth of topsoil. Record the observations in your notebook.

3b. Visual Observations

Soluble Salt

MATERIALS:

○ Site assessment notebook

ESTIMATED TIME: 5 minutes

Look (particularly near walks and parking areas in early spring) for white powder that has precipitated from the soil surface. Deicing salts linger and can cause damage to plants. There are other sources for soluble salts, but it is difficult to see them. If you suspect a problem, more extensive lab tests may be warranted. Record observations in your notebook.

USING WHAT YOU FOUND IN THIS STEP

The percentages of sand, silt, and clay can indicate which component is most dominant. A soil that has a high percentage of sand is sandy; high silt is silty; and high clay is clayey.

In soil, textural type is a description of relative proportion of particle sizes. Many of our garden soils are some variation of loam—some are moderately fine, some are medium and others are moderately coarse. The variations come from the amount of sand, clay, or silt that the loamy soil contains.

In some areas, garden soils have soil textures other than loam. Silty soils feel somewhat like flour. Clayey soils have predominately small or fine particle size, but they will clump up easily and, when wet, will feel like you can roll and mold them like…well, clay. Sandy soils are coarse to the touch. The textural differences give an indication of drainage potential, ability to hold nutrients, and ability for plant roots to develop. Sandy soils drain well, but hold nutrients poorly; clayey soils drain poorly, but retain nutrients well. Clayey soils (and, to some extent, silty soils) compact more easily than sandy soils, making it more difficult for roots to develop.

Use the simplified soil texture triangle to determine the soil textural type. Find the percentage of clay, silt, and sand from your soil sedimentation test.

Mark the point of each percentage on this triangle. From the percentage clay number, draw a straight line from it, left to right, parallel to the bottom of the triangle. From the percentage silt number, draw a straight line from it to the bottom left, parallel to the left side of the triangle. From the percentage sand number, draw a straight line from it to the top left, parallel to the right side of the triangle. Where the three lines meet is the general category of your soil textural type.

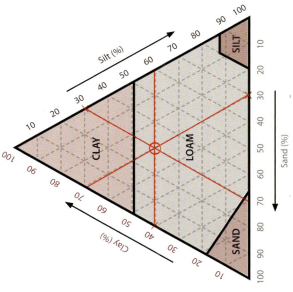

Simplified Soil Texture Triangle. The example is for a soil that is 40% clay, 30% silt, and 30% sand.

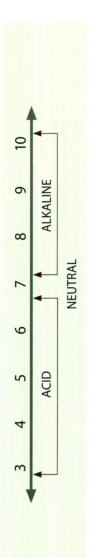

The pH scale.

The soil shown in the photo on page 35 is 50% clay, 5% silt, and 45% sand. So, it is a clayey soil type. Using the results of your sedimentation test, locate your soil on the triangle. In your notebook, record whether the soil is clayey, loamy, sandy, or silty. For a more precise soil textural classification, refer to the USDA soil textural class triangle in the glossary.

Soil is what it is. Only in extreme cases is it unable to support plant growth. You may garden or landscape with whatever soil you have and make choices accordingly. For instance, if you have a soil high in clay, you may choose plants that tolerate poorly drained soils. Or you may add organic matter to your soil, which can help improve drainage.

Organic matter also improves sandy soil, helping it retain more water and nutrients. Or you could choose to grow plants that tolerate drought and low nutrient levels.

Organic matter, an important component of healthy soils, breaks down continuously, and needs to be replenished. One source of organic matter is topsoil sold in bags or by the truckload. Other sources are compost, well-rotted manure, or peat moss. All are mixed into existing soils. Incorporate only thoroughly composted or decomposed manure into the soil. Otherwise, it will compete with plants for nutrients as it decomposes.

The results of a pH test indicate on a scale of 0–14 whether your soil is acidic, neutral, or alkaline — the lower the number, the more acidic the soil. A pH of 5.5 is 10 times more acid than a 6.5 pH, a 4.5 pH is 100 times more acidic than a 6.5 pH. An acid soil will not burn people, pets, or plants.

The soil pH is important information for plant selection and site preparation. Most plants prefer a soil pH between 6 and 7. Rhododendrons, azaleas, hollies, and blueberries, prefer a pH between 4.5–5.8. Changing pH can be difficult, especially after planting. Lowering pH is harder than raising it.

Lime is used to reduce the acidity (raise the pH) of soil. Sulfur is used to increase acidity (decrease pH). Application rates are based on recommendations from a soil test. Soils tend to resist pH change and amendments may need to be added each year. If the pH is extremely different from the new planting's needs, it may be necessary to start amending the soil a year before you plant. Check with your Cooperative Extension office for advice on altering soil pH in your area.

In this step, the soil sample used to measure the pH was a mixture of samples taken from around the site. When planning plantings for a subsection of the site, test for pH and nutrients to determine if soil characteristics are favorable.

Instead of trying to change the pH, consider other options. You can choose a plant that will thrive without changing the soil's pH. For example,

Dumping

L ook for signs that paint, oil, or gasoline have been dumped on the property. Signs may include only weeds growing in an area or soil that is completely bare. Observations like this are best made occasionally over time rather than just once. Plants may not grow in an area if dumping has been excessive.

Record observations in your notebook.

rhododendron refers to shrubs with large clusters of flowers.

Sugar maple – *Acer saccharum*
White pine – *Pinus strobes*

FOR FURTHER READING

Building Soils for Better Crops, 3rd Edition, Fred Magdoff and Harold van Es. Sustainable Agriculture Publications, Waldorf, MD 2010. You can purchase a paper copy or download a pdf of the book at **http://www.sare.org/Learning-Center/Books**

Composting to Reduce the Waste Stream, NRAES-43, Robert Kozlowski, NRAES, Ithaca, NY, 1991. Purchase online at **http://palspublishing.cals.cornell.edu/**

Secrets to Great Soil (Storey's Gardening Skills Illustrated), by Elizabeth Stell, Workman Publishing Co, New York, 1998.

Soil Science Simplified, 4th Edition, by Helmut Kohnke and D.P. Franzmeier, Waveland Press, Prospect Heights, Illinois, 1995. Includes technique for estimating soil texture by manipulating it in the hand.

Start with the soil: The Organic Gardener's Guide to Improving Soil for Higher Yields, More Beautiful Flowers, and a Healthy, Easy-Care Garden, Grace Gershuny, Rodale Press, Emmaus, PA 1995.

PLANTS MENTIONED IN STEP 8

The common name is followed by the scientific name and then additional information if needed.

Austrian pine – *Pinus australis*

Blueberry – *Vaccinium* sp. – there are about 16 species that may be considered blueberries. The most common blueberry plants are *Vaccinium corymbosum* (highbush blueberry) and *Vaccinium angustifolia* (lowbush blueberry).

Currant – common currants grown in the U.S.A are red currants (*Ribes rubrum*) red currant and white currants (*Ribes glandulosum*)

Gooseberry – *Ribes uva-crispa*

Honey locust – *Gleditsia triacanthos*

Pin oak – *Pinus palustris*

Red oak – *Quercus rubrum*

Rhododendron – *Rhododendron* sp. – a genus of more than nine-hundred species, which includes plants with the common names of azalea and rhododendron. When used as a common name,

salt-tolerant plants or install a burlap fence to shield against splashing road salt. A few examples of salt-tolerant trees are honey locust, Austrian pine, and red oak. Trees that do not tolerate soluble salts include sugar maple, white pine, and pin oak.

Soil Health

There is growing interest worldwide in improving soil in all its aspects, especially as it affects the economy, including farming. While traditional soil science has focused on soil chemistry and the physical characteristics of soil, there is now more focus on the biology of soil, including its microorganisms. The biology of soil plays a great role in improving plant productivity and environmental quality. Soil health emphasizes the integration of biological, chemical, and physical measures of soil quality. Awareness of this will help home gardeners think of soil as a dynamic plant growing medium instead of just dirt.

instead of lowering the pH for blueberry plants that prefer a pH of 4.5 and 5.8, choose currant or gooseberry plants that thrive in soil with a pH of 6.5. Or, you can create a raised bed and bring in the soil with the right pH and other factors to grow the plants you desire.

If you have found evidence of soluble salts near driveways, sidewalks, or roads, flush salted planting areas with water in the spring. Use plant-friendly deicing salts or coarse sand for traction during winter. For plantings near roadsides, choose

Visit **http://www.hort.cornell.edu/site/** *for a link to the web sites below, and all web sites mentioned in this book.*

Organic Matter

www.gardening.cornell.edu/factsheets/orgmatter/index.html

Using Organic Matter in the Garden
From Cornell Cooperative Extension by Charles Mazza, Sally Cunningham, and Ellen Harrison.

www.extension.oregonstate.edu/catalog/pdf/ec/ec1561.pdf

Improving Garden Soils with Organic Matter
From Oregon State University by Neil Bell, Dan M. Sullivan, Linda J. Brewer, and John Hart.

Salt-tolerant Trees

www.hort.cornell.edu/uhi/outreach/recurbtree/pdfs/11salttol.pdf

From *Recommended Urban Trees: Site Assessment and Tree Selection for Stress Tolerance*, Urban Horticulture Institute, Cornell University, 2009.

Salt Sensitive Trees

www.hort.cornell.edu/uhi/outreach/recurbtree/pdfs/12saltsens.pdf

From *Recommended Urban Trees: Site Assessment and Tree Selection for Stress Tolerance*, Urban Horticulture Institute, Cornell University, 2009.

Soil Basics

http://blogs.cornell.edu/horticulture/soil-basics/

From the Cornell Garden Based Learning, Department of Horticulture, Cornell University.

Soil Health

http://soilhealth.cals.cornell.edu

Cornell Soil Health website. Includes a soil health assessment manual—primarily for farmers, but instructive to others. From Cornell University.

http://www.soilhealth.com/

Includes a section that explains how soils are alive. From the University of Western Australia.

Slopes

Plantings on this steep slope will reduce erosion and stabilize the bank.

WHY IS THIS IMPORTANT?

Not all properties are level. If your property is level, you can skip this step.

On some properties there are slopes that noticeably change the topography, while on others the slopes are so gradual that they could be overlooked on first inspection. As you gain more experience, you will find books, articles, internet references, or neighbors referring to precautions when planting on sloped ground. Some trees, shrubs, herbaceous perennials (groundcovers, wildflowers, and a mixture of perennial plants) and annuals are more suited to flat land than to sloped areas.

Where slopes exist on a property, it helps to note their location and quantify their steepness. There are considerations for clearly sloped areas that are different from relatively level ground. The steeper the slope, the more challenging it will be to manage over the years.

Steep and very steep slopes may pose erosion problems after rain or gradually over time. Slopes may affect drainage and decisions about which

plants to select. Sometimes a plant's root system is too shallow to persist on sloped land. Steep slopes require plants with deeper, soil stabilizing roots for success, and to prevent erosion.

And . . . what is planted on the flat land adjacent to the slope bottom may be affected by what is happening on the slope. Soil washing down may nearly bury a plant or puddling may occur. Avoid these issues on severely sloped land by accounting for slopes in the overall landscape design. A continuously wet site at the base of a steep slope is a prime location for unwanted water-loving weeds that are difficult to eradicate. If a steep slope can be made less of a sliding board for soil and water, it can go a long way to improving the long-term success of the landscape and gardens beneath it.

ACTIVITIES

1. Measuring steepness of slopes.

(adapted from interview with Michael Circeo, civil engineer, Roanoke, Virginia)

MATERIALS

- Ball of string or cord
- Crayon or waterproof marker
- Foot ruler
- Yardstick
- Sketch from Step 1
- Small bubble level
- Helper
- Site assessment notebook

ESTIMATED TIME: 30 minutes for each slope

Estimating the steepness of a slope is simple and easy if done with a helper. When selecting plants, it helps to know if a slope is gradual or a steep. Some will make a quick estimate of slope angle, but it is surprising how difficult it is to "eyeball it." This is one task that might first be done by an experienced professional. But, it is a doable task for gardeners to repeat, especially those who want to do a thorough site assessment.

You will have to do several measurements on a slope that varies. Record the data collected and calculations in your notebook.

1. On a cord 25 feet long, mark every 12 inches with your crayon or marker. If you need more than 25 feet of cord for this activity, you have a gradually sloped site.

2. Set up the yardstick at the base of a slope you are measuring. The yardstick's 3-foot length will be a constant factor.

3. Tie the marked cord to the very top of the yardstick so that the full first foot is tied around the yardstick.

4. Pull the remaining cord tightly toward the slope. Be sure that it is as level horizontally as possible. Use a bubble level to assure that it is level.

5. While one person holds the cord down on the slope, the other person measures the cord length. The shorter the horizontal length, the steeper the slope.

6. Use the following formula to calculate the slope:

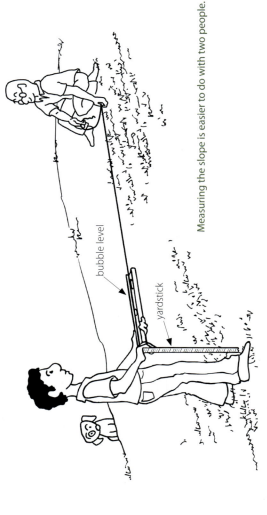

bubble level

yardstick

Measuring the slope is easier to do with two people.

Add codes to your sketch to mark sloped areas. For example use *MS* for moderate slopes, *SS* for steep slopes, and *VSS* for very steep slopes. Add the codes to the sketch's legend. Also mark the slope's percentage.

2. Visual observations on erosion.

MATERIALS

○ Sketch started in Step 1
○ Site assessment notebook

ESTIMATED TIME: 5–10 minutes and ongoing observations

$$\% \text{ slope} = 100 \times [\text{vertical (ft.)} \div \text{horizontal (ft.)}]$$

7. Use this chart to determine the general category for your slope.

Slope		Horizontal length (ft.) of cord
Very steep	> 50%	< 6 ft.
Steep	50–20%	6–15 ft.
Moderate	20–12.5%	15–24 ft.
Gradual	12.5–3%	24–100 ft.
Flat	< 3%	> 100 ft.

The symbol < means "less than"; > means "greater than."

plant ground covers, other herbaceous perennials, and/or deep-rooted trees or shrubs to slow the process of erosion and anchor the soil.

The choices of ground covers and herbaceous perennials are much broader for a gradual slope. A few plants successfully used on gentle or even moderate slopes are creeping phlox, carpet bugle, and cranesbill. Almost all types of shrubs will gain a foothold on a gradual or moderate slope, if protected for a few years from gushing water that can dislodge new plantings. Mulching helps, especially in the early years.

On steep slopes, shrub ground covers, such as cotoneaster, Arnold dwarf (spreading) forsythia, Siberian cypress, or dwarf cutleaf stephanandra, or deep-rooted herbaceous perennials, such as daylilies, are a few examples of ground covers that could be used. A sloped area of 10 × 25 feet (250 sq. ft.) may need as few as twenty to twenty-five plants (such as shrubs that spread widely) to a hundred or more plants (such as herbaceous perennials that fill in slowly and do not spread very much). While difficult to establish on steep slopes because of soil erosion, daffodils, which multiply and spread over years, can be a welcome burst of color in the spring. Planting steep slopes with ground covers that have shallow roots, such as creeping thyme, sweet woodruff, or sedges, can be very unstable as the root system cannot hold onto the slope when there

A retaining wall with drainage pipes is a practical solution for a very steep slope.

Terraces hold back the soil on a steep slope and create a flat planting space on the top.

- ☐ Determine the extent and severity of soil erosion. Record observations in your notebook.
- ☐ On your sketch, note the presence and size of eroded gullies.

Factors that affect soil erosion include: rainfall intensity, quantity, and runoff; wind; slope length and gradient; amount of stabilizing plant material or other erosion control practices; the infiltration rate; and the structural stability of the soil.

USING WHAT YOU FOUND IN THIS STEP

Mowing lawns on steep slopes can be dangerous and they need to be mowed regularly. If you have steep or very steep slopes, using a walk-behind or riding mower is a safety hazard because the mower may tip over. With gradual slopes, lawn mowing is much less risky.

Instead of a lawn on a steep slope, consider a planting of woody shrubs and/or trees or a planting of herbaceous perennials that can thrive on steep slopes. Once established, they generally require less maintenance than lawns (except weed control and occasional pruning, of course). And, they are safer because you are not running a mower over the slope every week.

Decide what kind of planting you will need on your slopes. With moderate and steeper slopes, is excessive rain or water runoff. In all cases, while plants are being established on steep slopes, use mulch to prevent erosion. It may be necessary to refresh the mulch regularly over the several years it takes to establish full cover in a ground cover planting.

In addition to the planting options described above, stabilize very steep slopes to avoid excessive erosion by:

☐ Building a retaining wall with drainage pipes, which will allow you to reshape the steepness into a gentler slope.

☐ Creating a series of terraces horizontally along the slope and planting on the flat surface of each terrace.

PLANTS MENTIONED IN STEP 9

The common name is followed by the scientific name and then additional information if needed.

Arnold dwarf (spreading) forsythia – *Forsythia* × *intermedia* 'Arnold Dwarf'. The common name is technically Arnold dwarf forsythia; the word spreading in parentheses is inserted to emphasize its spreading habit here.

Carpet bugle – *Ajuga reptans*. Also known as bugleweed or bugle.

Cotoneaster – *Cotoneaster* sp. – a genus of over 100 species.

Cranesbill – *Geranium* sp. – a genus of over 200 species and more cultivars. Sometimes referred to as hardy geraniums to distinguish them from the widely grown annual geraniums in the genus *Pelargonium*.

Creeping phlox – *Phlox stolonifera*. Other phlox species – *Phlox sublata* (Moss Phlox, Moss Pink, Mountain Phlox), the hybrid between the two, *Phlox* × *procumbens* (Millstream phlox), or *Phlox nivalis* (Trailing phlox) all are also creeping in habit and suitable on slopes.

Creeping thyme – *Thymus serphyllum*

Daffodil – *Narcissus* sp. – there are 13 categories (called divisions) of Narcissus, with with at least 50 speies and over 1,300 hybrids. Some are called narcissus, some jonquils.

Daylily – *Hemerocallis* sp. – a highly hybridized genus, with thousands of cultivars.

Dwarf cutleaf stephanandra – (also called lace shrub) *Stephanandra incisa* 'Crispa'

Sedges – a family of plants with over a hundred genera. The family name is Cyperaceae; perhaps the most common genus of sedge for garden use is *Carex* sp. Although not technically a grass, it has the appearance of grass plants.

Siberian cypress – *Microbiota decussata*

Sweet woodruff – *Galium odoratum* or *Asperula odoratum* (synonym)

FOR FURTHER READING

Visit **http://www.hort.cornell.edu/site/** *for links to the web sites below and all web sites mentioned in this book.*

Building Retaining Walls

http://hometime.com/Howto/projects/retain/rtn_1.htm
From HOMETIME.com

Deciduous Woody Ground Covers

www.hort.cornell.edu/uhi/outreach/pdfs/dwgc.pdf
From the Urban Horticulture Institute, Department of Horticulture, Cornell University

Herbaceous Ground Covers

http://ohioline.osu.edu/hyg-fact/1000/1648.html
From The Ohio State University by Jack Kerrigan and David Edenfield

Wildlife Interference

WHY IS THIS IMPORTANT?

If you discover plant damage caused by unwanted animals you have choices. You can decide to tolerate the damage, peacefully coexisting with the animals, or you can turn it into a battle of wits. Animals that typically cause damage to plants include deer, squirrels, rabbits, chipmunks, groundhogs, and voles. Identifying wildlife that exists on your property will take observations over time. Animals leave signs, and with a little experience, you will be able to identify the culprit.

Animal populations change. An increase in population could come about if an animal's natural habitat has been altered by new construction or if weather and habitat conditions were right for an increase in offspring. That is called an increase in animal pressure and associated damage. A decrease in animal pressure could occur if disease, summer drought, or a severe winter affects wildlife abundance. Drought reduces the natural food sources for wildlife. Severe winter increases the animal's energy requirements and deep snow limits their access to food.

You won't always see the animal munching in your garden. Sometimes the damage is done at night or when there are no people around. Sometimes you can tell by the plant damage what critter was responsible, but often you cannot. Considering animal pressure when planning a new or modified landscape will improve your chances for success. Talk with neighbors. If they experience wildlife damage, you may see the same critters on your property.

source: © Paul Curtis

A vole eating an apple.

ACTIVITIES

(adapted from communication with Dr. Paul Curtis, Department of Natural Resources, Cornell University)

1. Find out if you have voles.

MATERIALS

- Fresh apples
- Knife
- Pieces of roofing shingle or boards
- Site assessment notebook

ESTIMATED TIME: 15–20 minutes and one day waiting time

Cut a whole apple vertically through the core into 14–16 slices. Locate areas in planting beds or gardens with thick mulch, weed, or grass cover. Meadow voles leave evidence of runways at the ground surface in areas with thick cover. Pine voles have 1- to 2-inch burrow openings to underground tunnel systems. Place apple slices in a runway or near a burrow entrance. Cover with pieces of wood or roofing shingle about one foot square to entice the voles to eat with protection from predators and to prevent the apples from being eaten by larger animals. Place apple slices about 10 to 15 feet apart in the garden area you are monitoring. Check the apple slices 24 hours later. In your notebook, record where you detected apples eaten by voles.

2. Observing for deer damage

MATERIALS

○ Site assessment notebook

ESTIMATED TIME: 10 minutes

Examine woody ornamentals for evidence of deer feeding damage. Deer have no upper incisors, so they leave ragged, torn edges on leaves and branches. Examine plants that deer favor, such as yews, arborvitae, rhododendron, and fruit trees for evidence of torn limbs or shoot tips up to 6 feet from the ground. If deer are abundant in the neighborhood, browse lines will be evident on evergreens. Record observations in your notebook.

What about Moles?

Moles are often unfairly blamed for vole damage. Moles eat insects (grubs, beetle larvae) and worms; voles eat plants. Moles and voles are both about 5 to 7 inches long, but moles have very prominent pointed snouts and spade-shaped front feet for digging. Vole snouts are more rounded and their feet are more mouse-like.

Moles are beneficial because they: (1) eat undesirable grubs and insects; (2) move soil around to increase aeration; (3) bring organic matter farther down into the soil; and (4) bring subsoil up, delivering nutrients to the root zone. Some homeowners object to the molehills and shallow tunnels that moles create. Molehills are circular mounds with round ripple marks made by new loads

of soil pushed to the surface. Shallow tunnels create a heaved surface, which makes it difficult to mow the lawn. Burrowing can damage grass roots by exposing them to air. A mole's den area has irregular chambers

source: National Science Foundation

Eastern mole.

connected with runways, 1 to 1.5 feet beneath the soil surface. Deep runways also lead from the mole's den to its hunting grounds. Eventually the unused tunnels become filled with settling soil, especially after heavy rains.

Chipmunks may also excavate tunnels in lawns, but the tunnels do not have obvious mounds of earth on the surface, and their deep tunnels are not visible at the surface. Chipmunks prefer burrowing near rock walls and rock gardens and their tunnel systems may be completely hidden.

harvesting or damaging all your cherries, strawberries, blueberries, raspberries, and other soft, small fruits. It may also protect soft vegetables like tomatoes. Not much protects your garden from squirrels.

Chipmunks are one of many small animals, such as rabbits, squirrels, and groundhogs that may interfere with gardening. There are no easy activities to determine whether chipmunks are present. Careful observation is the only site assessment tool.

Damage by your own or your neighbors' cats and dogs is a different issue. Often the damage from dogs, for instance, comes from their habit of digging holes, which disturbs plant roots. Other dogs do damage to the garden by running over

Chipmunks can damage gardens by burrowing under patios and walls or eating bulbs and seedlings.

If deer damage to shrubs is severe, surround plants with a wire cage or bird netting attached to stakes. In extreme cases, it may be necessary to erect 8 foot high fences surrounding your property or specialized garden, such as an orchard or vegetable garden. Lower fences, properly installed, are sufficient to deter rabbits and groundhogs.

Repellents are an alternative to netting. While they work for a while, they don't last forever. Generally, repellents that work by emitting strong smells, such as rotten eggs, are better than those that deter by adding an unpleasant taste to the plant.

In many cases, dogs contained within an invisible fence keep deer away. Dogs need to patrol day and night because most feeding occurs after dark. There are a few plants that deer rarely eat, such as boxwood, daffodils, spruce, or pachysandra. However, there is no definitive list of deer-resistant plants. Many lists are distributed with local observations, but none are foolproof.

In this step, you assessed if voles and deer pose a challenge for your landscape or garden. The two activities in this step do not determine if other animals patrol your property. Some animals pass through, do no detectable damage, and may be welcome on your property.

Birds and squirrels compete with you for ripening fruit. Bird netting may help to keep birds from

Pete looks perplexed as he discovers deer damage on his arborvitae. Where was Herb? Dogs are supposed to keep deer away!

USING WHAT YOU FOUND IN THIS STEP

No plants are animal-proof. An animal's desire for a plant is dependent on the foraging pressure or how desperate the animal is for food. Talk with neighbors about what they have observed. It is better not to assume that you have animals just because they are on your neighbors' property. It would be equally shortsighted to assume that no hungry animals visit your property.

If you have a small number of voles, ordinary mousetraps may help reduce their population.

plants; straight paths give dogs a chance to run and minimize garden damage.

Plants Mentioned in Step 10

The common name is followed by the scientific name and then additional information if needed.

Arborvitae – *Thuja occidentalis*

Boxwood – *Buxus* sp. – a genus of over 70 species; the most common is *Buxus sempervirens*.

Daffodil – *Narcissus* sp. – there are 13 categories (called divisions) of Narcissus, with at least 50 species and over 1,300 hybrids. Some are called narcissus, some jonquils.

Pachysandra – *Pachysandra* sp. – a genus of four or five species; the most commonly planted one is *Pachysandra terminalis*, also known as Japanese spurge.

Rhododendron – *Rhododendron* sp. – a genus of more than 900 species, which includes plants with the common names of azalea and rhododendron. When used as a common name, rhododendron refers to shrubs with large clusters of flowers.

Spruce – *Picea* sp. – a genus of about 35 species

Yew – *Taxus* sp. – a genus of about 9 species; the most common are *Taxus baccata* (common yew) and *Taxus cuspidata* (Japanese yew).

For Further Reading

Visit **http://www.hort.cornell.edu/site/** *for links to the web sites below and all web sites mentioned in this book.*

Moles

http://pubs.cas.psu.edu/FreePubs/pdfs/uh084.pdf
From Penn State University

Wildlife Damage Management and Control

wildlifecontrol.info/pubs/Pages/default.aspx
Links to online publications from Northeast states related to wildlife damage management and control.

http://icwdm.org
Research-based information on how to responsibly handle wildlife damage problems. From the Internet Center for Wildlife Damage Management.

http://www.extension.org/category/human-wildlife_relations
Articles about human-wildlife relations. Option to ask an expert questions.

Deer-browsing damage on arborvitae.

Existing Plants

WHY IS THIS IMPORTANT?

Whether you are assessing a new property or one you have had for years, it helps to know which shrubs, trees, ground covers, vines, and other perennial plants are on the property. To make changes or improvements, you need to decide the fate of existing plants. Some will be mature and in good condition; others will be in poor condition and a liability. Some will be in good condition, but were planted where they cannot be sustained. The existing plants will challenge you to make decisions based on preferences, maintenance needs, and new plans.

Without going through this step carefully, you run the risk of overlooking, forgetting, or being surprised at the presence of plants as you implement your plan. They will be in the way instead of what they are now—one more site assessment factor.

It is useful to know the size and location of trees on the property or near the property line. Densely-branched trees and leafed trees can block both sunlight and rain from reaching the area under the trees. As a tree matures, the root system expands competing with other plants for water and nutrients.

Planting under a tree is a risk. Measuring the tree height and canopy spread will help define the area that will be blocked from sunlight and rain.

The evergreen cherry laurel shrubs will need irrigation and fertilizing to stay in decent condition. They are competing for nutrients and water with the mature, 2-foot diameter (dbh) ornamental pear tree.

A canopy is a tree's mass of branches and leaves or needles. In many cases, the canopy is umbrella-shaped. In some cases, the widest part is at the bottom and tree is cone-shaped. Canopies can be dense, moderately dense, or open, depending on the species, age, and health of the tree.

A healthy tree has structural and feeder roots in balance with the branches, leaves, flowers, fruits, and seeds of the canopy. When in balance, the root system supplies the canopy with the water and nutrients needed to thrive without stress. An extensive tree canopy requires an extensive root system to support it structurally and biologically. For most trees, roots are concentrated in the upper three-feet of soil.

Construction activity around trees can severe roots. Removing soil when regrading to make the slope steeper may expose roots. Exposed roots may dry out and lose their ability to absorb water and nutrients. Adding soil to make the slope flatter might reduce the oxygen available to the roots. The root system depends on oxygen to function.

The more feeder roots are damaged by cutting, exposing, or burying them, the more likely the tree is to be stressed for nutrients, water, or oxygen. You may not observe this stress to the canopy right away, but it results in a slow reduction of vigor and eventually causes the tree to decline. If large roots are severed, the tree may not stand up to strong winds or floods. While root regeneration on healthy trees occurs, it might take years. In the meantime, the tree's health would be threatened.

ACTIVITIES

1. What plants are on the property? — The Plant Inventory

MATERIALS

- Marking tags with string attached
- Pencil, waterproof marker, or paint pen
- Clear tape
- Clipboard with lined paper
- Wooden shish kebab skewers or craft sticks (optional)
- Site assessment notebook

ESTIMATED TIME: Depends on the extent of the existing planting. Probably at least an hour to affix tags on an average yard. Identifying all plants, their condition, and fate may take much more time, depending on your knowledge. Since some plants are easier to identify at certain times of the year, it may take a year to identify all plants.

Marking tags are available at most stationery or office supply stores and they already have string attached. The tags can be any size or color you want, but small, white ones (about an inch square in size) with thin string to attach to a branch will do. Permanent plastic, wood, or metal plant labels are sold in garden centers.

This activity is designed for properties or study areas within a property that have widely spaced

Pete numbers and labels his plants.

permanent plants (trees, shrubs, herbaceous perennials). For densely planted areas, make separate maps as described in the sidebar.

Do the plant inventory throughout the year since some plants are easier to identify at certain times of year. For instance, herbaceous perennials can't be identified in winter but can be easily identified when flowering.

Annual flowers, herbs, and vegetables need not be recorded since annuals die off at the end of the growing season. If you don't know if something is an annual, include it. You can cross it off the list and remove the label in the fall if it's an annual.

Walk around your property with a stack of marking tags and sticks. Attach a tag to each plant even if you will be eliminating it in the future. Write a unique number on each tag. This will be used to key it to the plant inventory. For ground covers or herbaceous perennials, put a stick in the ground to hold the marking label.

Rain and other inclement weather can quickly damage marking tags, which may stay on the plants for months. To weatherproof, cover the label with clear tape after you number it.

Create a plant inventory by transferring the numbers to your notebook or a spreadsheet. If using paper, write in pencil since the information may change. Organizing the inventory into a table

Plant Inventory for Densely-Planted Areas

For flower beds, shrub plantings, or other areas densely-planted with perennial plants, it is not practical to tag every plant. Make a map for each densely-planted area and add a unique number for each planting at its approximate location.

Create a plant inventory on the map or in your site assessment notebook. Correlate the numbers on the map with the plantings in the inventory. For each planting, include the number, common name, scientific name, condition, fate (keep, move, renew, remove), and date of the decision. Take photos of the mapped area from different angles. Mark your sketch started in Step 1 with a code to remind you that you have a map of the area. For example, "M" for map. Add the code to the sketch's legend.

---

may make it easier to use, but the format is up to you. For each plant add the information you know to this point such as the:

- □ plant number
- □ common name of plant
- □ scientific name of plant, including cultivar name
- □ location—keep it brief (e.g., east side near sidewalk)
- □ size (trees only)—see Activity 2 below
- □ condition of plant (good, fair, poor)
- □ decision on what to do about the plant (keep, move, renew, remove)
- □ date of decision

Consider this activity a "work-in-progress." You may not know the scientific and cultivar names for all plants at first. You can fill in the names as you learn them. And, you may want to get a second opinion on the condition of the plant. As you learn more, you can add information to the plant inventory or change your initial decision on the fate of a plant.

Plants are usually named based on their flower and fruit structure. Leaf shape and appearance may be used in some books to narrow down large groups of plants with similar leaves. Each plant has a scientific name consisting of the genus and species. For example, *Acer saccharum* refers to sugar maple and *Acer palmatum* refers to Japanese maple. To speed up the inventory, use the common name of plants. Often a cultivar (cultivated variety) name also exists. If a nursery label is still on an existing plant, include the cultivar name.

With landscape plants, different cultivars of the same species and genus may have different, distinct characteristics such as dwarf, upright, horizontal, dense, disease resistant, or hardy. These characteristics can help you decide whether to keep, renew, move or remove a plant. Sometimes cultivars indicate flower-color differences.

Add marking tags to perennial noxious weeds such as bindweed, mugwort, nutsedge, Japanese knotweed, quackgrass, and healall and plan to eradicate them before landscape installation. Number the tags and use the same number to identify the plants in the inventory. For poison ivy, put a stake in the ground near the plant and tag it for identification and to alert others.

Become familiar with sapling trees that sprout from seeds sometimes in undesirable locations. Label trees such as Norway maple, mulberry, ash, and box elder. Remove them if they are in undesirable locations.

Needle disease on Austrian pine.

source: HGIC

The photo on the left shows a grade change around a trunk with no natural flare and small roots in the mulch and soil. The photo on the right shows a natural flare.

A Japanese Beetle and its damage to the leaves of an herbaceous perennial.

The Japanese maple above is in poor condition with more than half of its branches dying. It could be saved with severe drastic pruning, but given its prominent position, it should be removed and replaced. The Japanese maple (left) is in good condition.

In determining the condition of plants, consider indicators of poor health below. Examples of plant condition are shown on this page and the following page. The book *Broadleaved Shrubs and Shade Trees*, listed in the For Further Reading list at the end of this step, has over 400 pictures of plant conditions.

- ☐ Small, off-color leaves that drop early in the fall. Stress symptoms are often confused with diseases symptoms.

- ☐ Obvious evidence of disease.

- ☐ Obvious evidence of insect damage.

- ☐ Broken branches.

- ☐ Excessive suckers or string trimmer damage at the base of tree trunks. Suckers are small shoots (stems and leaves) that emerge from the base of a plant.

- ☐ Tree bark that has been split or stripped.

- ☐ Whether the flare of a tree trunk is visible, rather than covered with soil or mulch and. Tree trunks where the flare is not visible may have been planted too deeply or, soil or mulch may have been piled around the base of the trunk at a later time, making the tree susceptible to decline.

- ☐ Branches with tip dieback. If there is significant dieback, is it all on one side of the canopy, or is it on both sides? Where the same plant is in multiple places on the site, note whether they all exhibit the same symptoms.

source: HGIC

Surface roots under a shade tree.

Marginal leaf scorch on a Norway maple.

Heavily pruned the previous year, this redbud tree has a proliferation of new shoots or water sprouts emerging near the cut branches.

Girdling root on Kentucky coffee tree. Eventually, girdling roots can strangle a tree.

- Excessive surface rooting and girdling roots on trees.

- Marginal leaf scorch.

- Excessive movement of tree trunks. Test the stability of newly planted trees by gently rocking them. Roots may have disease or insect problems, trees could have been planted improperly, or the roots may not have established after transplanting.

- Abnormal growths such as gall. Plant gall is an abnormal, swollen growth of plant tissue and can be caused by various parasites, fungi, bacteria, mites, or insects.

- Witch's broom is a dense mass of tree twigs, with a common starting point, that resembles a witch's broom or a bird's nest. May be caused by either biological or environmental stresses.

- Water sprouts (new shoots) may proliferate near cut branches. Cutting back all but one shoot will prevent having too many branches in the future. If you want to eliminate growth in that area, remove all the new shoots.

There is no right or wrong way to assess the condition of plants. Try to be consistent in what you call good, fair, and poor. Use book and Internet references with good photographs, in addition to talking with knowledgeable friends, to identify the condition of plants on your property.

You do not need to diagnose the cause of the condition you notice. Noting the visual characteristics is enough. Local Cooperative Extension horticulture staff may be able to advise you. A specialist may help you determine if the cause is stress, disease, or insect related. Remember that stress occurs from environmental conditions such as inadequate or excessive water, temperature, nutrients, or light.

2a. How big are the trees?
Tree Height and Canopy Spread

MATERIALS
- Yardstick
- Tape measure
- Pencil
- Site assessment notebook

ESTIMATED TIME: 10 minutes per tree

☐ Place a yardstick vertically against the trunk and step back so that the whole tree is in your sight. While holding a pencil at arm's length, line up the top of the yardstick with the tip of the pencil.

☐ Using your thumbnail, mark the base of the yardstick on the pencil. Now you have a ruler. Sighting up the tree, determine how many "rulers" fit into the tree.

☐ Multiply this number by the length of the yardstick (3 feet) for a height approximation.

☐ Look at the canopy and mark it's left and right limit on the ground. Use the tape measure to estimate the spread of the tree's canopy.

☐ Note whether the canopy on each tree is dense, moderately dense, or open. Try to be consistent.

Include your findings in the plant inventory.

While not an accurate measurement, the procedure does give an approximate tree height and canopy spread, and it is better than guessing. If there are too many existing trees to measure each one, measure the tallest, the shortest, and one in the midsize range. From this you can estimate the height of the others. You can do the same to estimate the canopy spread of trees.

2b. How big are the trees?
Measuring Tree Trunk Diameter

MATERIALS
- Tape measure

ESTIMATED TIME: 3 minutes per tree

To determine the diameter of a tree trunk, start by measuring the circumference using a tape measure.

To determine the diameter of a tree trunk, start by measuring the circumference using a tape measure. Diameter is approximately one-third the circumference—circumference divided by 3.14. For large trees the circumference is measured at 4.5 ft. above ground. This is referred to as the diameter at breast height or dbh.

Another useful measurement is the caliper size. It is used by nurseries to describe trees they sell. Using the tape measure, measure the circumference of the existing tree about 6 inches above the ground. The caliper size is about one-third of the circumference. Record your findings in the plant inventory.

USING WHAT YOU FOUND IN THIS STEP

The plant inventory and decisions made on the fate of plants are key components to your garden and landscape plan. In the next step, this information will be combined with data collected in other steps to give you an overall view of your property. With all the information together, you can make final decisions on which plants to remove or move. In the Taking the Next Steps section, you will make a to-do list that prioritizes tasks, including removing, moving, or renewing plants.

As you consider the fate of existing plants, remember that some plants have deep roots. If you move or remove them, it may take the better part of a day to dig them up. Other plants may require professionals with specialized equipment to move or remove them. Those plants you decide to renew may need extensive pruning, staking, trellising, or reshaping. You can do the work yourself, hire a landscape contractor, or hire a local teenager.

Poorly-placed plants may have to be removed. As trees grow to mature sizes, they take up more space and create more shade. Factor that in as you plan. With shrubs and woody vines, however, it is possible to manage their size by judicious pruning.

A rule of thumb defines a tree protection zone as a circle around the trunk with 1 foot of radius for each inch of dbh. Avoid changing the grade or building walls, patios or other below-ground based construction projects in the tree protection zone. This rule-of-thumb is primarily for tree root protection. For instance, if you have a mature tree with a 12-inch dbh, avoid construction projects within 12 feet of the trunk. Digging within this circle will do damage to the roots. In this example, tree roots may spread out in a circle as far as 12 feet from the trunk of the tree. Vegetable gardens, where the soil may be tilled annually, are best sited outside of the tree protection zone. Plants with extensive roots such as shrubs, perennials, and vegetables, will find sites under and near a tree challenging because they are in direct competition with tree roots.

Even grass plants with relatively small roots may get spotty, with more and more bare spaces as a tree grows. Weeds, especially those that can tolerate dry, less fertile soil, may fill in.

Shallow-rooted, shade-tolerant ground covers, such as barrenwort or bishop's hat may survive for several years, but perhaps not permanently. Judicious watering and fertilizing helps, but the plan here is "less planting is better." In the long run, the best approach is to mulch under a tree.

If you must plant in a small space under a tree, keep it simple and at least avoid shrubs. Shallow rooted plants, like annuals or herbaceous perennials that can be replaced if necessary, are a compromise.

Tree roots from the other side of a fence or near a property line can affect plantings in the garden being assessed. When the tree is on a neighbor's property, you can't remove the tree, but don't ignore it either. It will influence your assessment and planning for the future.

PLANTS MENTIONED IN STEP 11

The common name is followed by the scientific name and then additional information if needed.

Austrian pine – *Pinus nigra*
Ash – *Fraxinus* sp. – a genus of about 50 species, about 6 of which are common in North America.

This mature spruce tree is in good condition but must be cut down or severely pruned. It is about 2 feet in diameter and is only 2 feet from the house. The roots will continue to grow and may damage the foundation.

Barrenwort or bishop's hat – *Epimedium* sp. – a genus of over 60 species, less than 10 of which are available in North America; the two most common are Epimedium grandiflorum and Epimedium rubrum, each with many cultivars.

Bindweed – *Convolvulus arvensis*. Also referred to as perennial morning glory, field bindweed or creeping jenny.

Box elder – *Acer negundo*

Cherry laurel – *Prunus laurocerasus*

Healall – *Prunella vulgaris*

Japanese knotweed – *Polygonum cuspidatum*

Japanese maple – *Acer palmatum*

Japanese knotweed (left) is an invasive weed. It can cover a streamside or field, choking everything else out and it takes several years to eradicate. It is so persistent that it re-sprouts from the base (right) even after judicious herbicidal treatment.

Tree Growth Rate

Quantify the last year's annual shoot extension by measuring the twig length between the growth tip (terminal bud) and the bud scar closest to the tip. Bud scars are markings on a stem (most noticeable in winter) that show the locations of previous terminal buds. The length between bud scars indicates one-years growth.

Measure several branches that receive daily sunlight and are within easy reach. Record measurements in your site assessment notebook. Greater than 6 inches a year is vigorous growth, 2 to 6 inches is moderate growth, and less than 2 inches is slow growth. A tree's rate of growth can be used to estimate its size in a few years. Trees reach a mature height when their growth rate slows or is imperceptible.

Indicate in the plant inventory whether a tree's growth is vigorous, moderate, or slow.

source: Susan Day

Bud scar marking on a red horse-chestnut tree. Not all bud scars are this obvious.

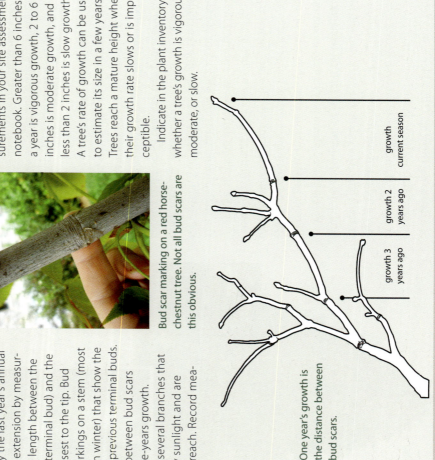

One year's growth is the distance between bud scars.

growth current season

growth 2 years ago

growth 3 years ago

Kentucky Coffee Tree – *Gymnocladus dioicus*

Mugwort – *Artemesia vulgaris*

Mulberry – *Morus alba*

Norway maple – *Acer platanoides*

Norway maple seedlings often grow in unwanted locations and should be removed while it is easy and inexpensive.

Nutsedge – *Cyperus esculentus* (yellow nutsedge) and *Cyperus rotundus* (purple nutsedge)

Pear Tree, Ornamental – *Pyrus calleryana*

Poison ivy – *Rhus radicans*

Quackgrass – *Elytrigia repens*

Redbud – *Cercis canadensis*. Also called Eastern redbud.

Red horsechestnut – *Aesculus* × *carnea* 'Briotii'

Spruce – *Picea sp.* The spruce shown in the photo is *Picea abies* (Norway spruce).

Sugar maple – *Acer saccharum*

FOR FURTHER READING

Use book and Internet references with good photographs, in addition to talking with knowledgeable friends and landscape professionals, to identify existing plants and their condition.

Broadleaved Shrubs and Shade Trees: Problems, Picture Clues, and Management Options, NRAES-183, by Mary Kay Malonoski and David Clement, NRAES, Ithaca, NY. Purchase online at **http://palspublishing.cals.cornell.edu/**

Herbaceous Perennial Plants: A Treatise on their Identification, Culture, and Garden Attributes, by Allan M. Armitage, Varsity Press, Athens, Georgia, 1989.

Manual of Woody Landscape Plants, 6th Edition, by Michael Dirr, Stipes Publishing, LLC, Champaign, Illinois, 2009. Useful for identifying trees, shrubs, and woody vines as well as their ultimate sizes and relative growth rates.

The Shrub Identification Book, by George Symonds, HarperCollins Publisher, New York, 1963.

Tree Finder: A Manual for the Identification of Trees by their Leaves, by May Theilgaard Watts, Nature Study Guild Publisher, Rochester, New York, 1998.

Tree ID Guide for Common Urban Trees in New York State and the Northeast. Urban Horticulture Institute, Cornell University. Order form available for this pocket-sized book at : **http://www.hort.cornell.edu/uhi/outreach/index.htm**

Weeds of the Northeast, by Richard H. Uva, Joseph C. Neal and Joseph M. DiTomaso. Cornell University Press, Ithaca, New York, 1997. Good guide to identifying weeds, including noxious weeds.

Visit **http://www.hort.cornell.edu/site/** *for links to the web sites below and all web sites mentioned in this book.*

Herbaceous Perennials

www.infography.com/content/246155002734.html Links to web pages with information about herbaceous perennials. From the Botanical Society of America

Tree Identification

http://www2.dnr.cornell.edu/ext/info/pubs/misc/KnowYourTrees.pdf An online version of *Know Your Trees*, by J. A. Cope and F. E. Winch, Jr., revised by E.A. Cope, Cornell University .

Putting It All Together

WHY IS THIS IMPORTANT?

By considering the characteristics of your site, you can generate a landscape and garden design that is informed and realistic. The information collected in the 11 steps provides a comprehensive view of the site. It is the basis for visualizing your future landscape and gardens. It is counterproductive to create a design without factoring in the site's opportunities and limitations. There are predetermined strengths and weaknesses on every property.

ACTIVITY

Record factors that describe your site.

MATERIAL

- Clipboard and pencil
- Notes taken during individual steps
- Sketch started in Step #1
- Plant inventory list from Step #11
- Maps of densely planted areas
- Site assessment notebook

ESTIMATED TIME: 20 minutes for each study area to collect information from previous steps

---

Fill out the Site Assessment Checklist on page 59 for your overall property. Then, fill out a separate checklist for each study area if you have them. A separate checklist may be needed if you are expanding into or refurbishing an area. A checklist is a reference—you can add new observations over time as you become more familiar with your site. Make copies of the blank checklist as needed. Store completed checklists in your note book.

USING WHAT YOU FOUND IN THIS STEP

The Site Assessment Checklist highlights important factors in your site assessment. You may be doing a site assessment for the entire property, or for an area where you are expanding or refurbishing. Whichever is your focus, limitations and assets on the site will stand out on the checklist. They are your own reality check. They act as a filter in making decisions later.

Throughout the site assessment, you have discovered much about your property. You gener-

---

ated notes in each step and three summaries of findings: a sketch, a plant inventory, and…now a checklist.

Property sketch includes:

- ☐ Size of area
- ☐ Direction of light
- ☐ Hardiness, microclimatic, and frost factors
- ☐ Location of:
  - Compacted-soil spots
  - Densely planted areas that have been mapped
  - Dry spots
  - Eroded areas
  - Heat and dryer vents
  - Obstructions
  - Outlets
  - Paths
  - Property signs
  - Poorly drained spots
  - Right-of-way
  - Septic tank and leach field
  - Sloped areas
  - Well

– Wet spots
– Windy spots
– Unsafe or hazardous spots

Plant inventory includes:

☐ Existing plants
☐ Condition of each
☐ Fate of each
☐ Maps and photos of densely planted areas if prepared
☐ Tree size
☐ Trees rate of growth

The Site Assessment Checklist includes information about:

☐ Climate
☐ Obstructions
☐ Soil and topography
☐ Wildlife
☐ Plants

What you have discovered in the 12 Steps, many gardeners have discovered over a longer period of time. Sometimes they learned intuitively. Sometimes they learned from mistakes—like ignoring, not realizing, or defying the unique physical conditions of the property. Or, footing a large bill because inappropriate trees, shrubs, and woody vines have become safety hazards or matured in places that could not support them.

FOR FURTHER READING

The Tree Care Primer, by Christopher Roddick with Beth Hanson, Brooklyn Botanic Garden All-Region Guides, Brooklyn, New York, 2007. Includes a chapter titled "The Perfect Match: The Right Tree in the Right Place"

Trees in the Urban Landscape: Site Assessment, Design, and Installation, by Peter Trowbridge and Nina L. Bassuk, John Wiley & Sons, Inc., Hoboken, New Jersey, 2004.

Visit **http://www.hort.cornell.edu/site/** *for a link to the web site below and all web sites mentioned in this book.*

Checklist for Site Assessment

www.hort.cornell.edu/uhi/outreach/recurbtree/pdfs/04sitelist.pdf
From *Recommended Urban Trees: Site Assessment and Tree Selection for Stress Tolerance*, Urban Horticulture Institute, Department of Horticulture, Cornell University, 2009.

Site Assessment Checklist
(make copies as needed)

Date _____ Location _____ Size (FROM STEP 1) _____

OBSTRUCTIONS

Below ground (FROM STEP 2):
☐ utilities shown on sketch ☐ irrigation system shown on sketch

Above-ground (FROM STEP 2):
☐ overhead wires (estimated height _____) shown on sketch

LOCAL CLIMATE

Sunlight levels (FROM STEP 3):
☐ full sun (6 hrs. or more) ☐ partial sun or filtered light ☐ shade

USDA hardiness zone (FROM STEP 4): __ 7 _ 6 _ 5 _ 4 _ 3 _ 2
last spring frost _____ first fall frost _____

Microclimatic factors (FROM STEP 4):
☐ reflected heat load ☐ frost pocket ☐ locations shown on sketch
☐ climate moderated ☐ rain shadow

Wind (FROM STEP 5):
☐ overall windy site ☐ windy in isolated sections ☐ relatively calm
☐ windy locations shown on sketch

SOIL FACTORS

Compaction (FROM STEP 6):
☐ compacted ☐ partially compacted ☐ compacted areas shown on sketch

Drainage characteristics (FROM STEP 7): ☐ wet ☐ well-drained ☐ dry
☐ wet or dry areas shown on sketch

Infiltration rating (FROM STEP 7): ☐ poor ☐ moderate ☐ good ☐ excessive

Percolation rating (FROM STEP 7): ☐ poor ☐ moderate ☐ excessive

Texture (FROM STEP 8): ☐ clayey ☐ loamy ☐ sandy ☐ silty

Soil pH (FROM STEP 8) _____

OBSERVATIONS

☐ unsafe areas (FROM STEP 1)
☐ recent construction (FROM STEP 6)
☐ clods with gray color or foul odor (FROM STEP 7)
☐ low lying spots that collect rain water (FROM STEP 7)
☐ topsoil was removed (FROM STEP 8) ☐ excessive salt usage (FROM STEP 8)
☐ soil contamination (FROM STEP 8) ☐ erosion (FROM STEP 9)

Slopes (FROM STEP 9): ☐ very steep ☐ steep ☐ moderate
☐ gradual or flat ☐ sloped areas shown on sketch

Interference from wildlife (FROM STEP 10): ☐ serious and obvious concerns
☐ marginal concerns to track ☐ not a problem now

Existing plants (FROM STEP 11):
_____ total number of trees _____ total number of shrubs
☐ presence of noxious weeds
☐ presence of plants that may indicate poorly drained spots (FROM STEP 7)

Taking the Next Steps

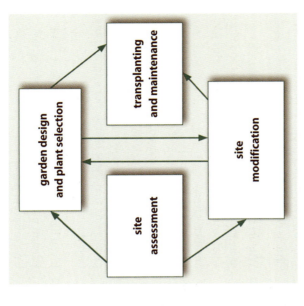

Site assessment precedes garden design, plant selection, site modification, and transplanting/maintenance

Now that you have assessed the site, the next steps are an action plan and, ultimately, creating your home landscape. To begin the action plan, ask yourself:

- What are my goals for the landscape and gardens over the next 5–20 years?
- What will I need to do to achieve my goals?

To get started, do three things. (1) list your long range goals in your site assessment notebook (2) draw a draft design that includes the garden and landscape areas you want and (3) generate a to-do list of projects to achieve those goals.

The draft landscape design will be refined over time, but it gives you a start. It includes goals in graphic form. The design process will be far more interesting if you keep the limiting factors in mind and seize the opportunities that the site assessment revealed. To start the draft, use the sketch made in Step 1 to make an outline of the property. The drawing on the next page is an example of how you can translate site assessment factors into

a draft design. While you may not be ready to name plants for each location, eventually you will. Select plants based on site limitations and assets as well as goals shown in the draft design. Matching plantings to the site's characteristics will help you create sustainable and easier-to-care-for landscapes and gardens.

To generate a list of projects, review the information amassed in the site assessment's discovery process. To paraphrase the well-known serenity prayer, written by theologian Reinhold Niebuhr in 1943, for the site assessment process, accept the unchangeable factors, change what you can, and hope you are wise enough to know the difference.

In your notebook, start by making a list of site factors that cannot be changed. Here are some examples.

- The size of the property, and the size of alcoves or extra spaces in an odd-shaped property, won't change.
- The hardiness zone is also a fixed factor. Consider it when selecting plants. While you may

be able to take advantage of microclimates or create them with fences, walls, or windbreaks, your hardiness zone can not be altered.

60

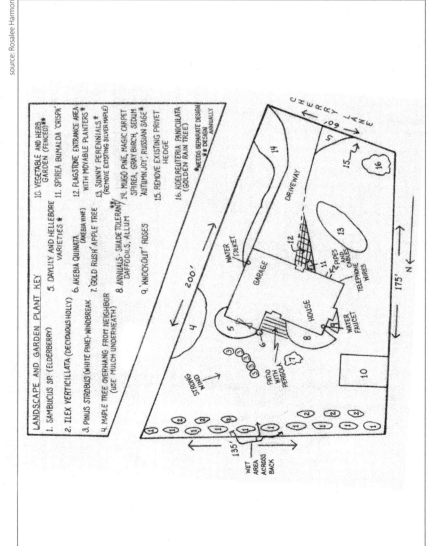

source: Rosalee Harmon

A landscape design can account for site variations. You can draw it yourself or hire professional landscape designers.

- Light can be a fixed factor. Morning sun comes in from the east, afternoon sun from the west. On the north side of the house, it is always shady. Unobstructed southern sunlight is full sun. Sunlight or shade can only be created or altered when structures are added or trees grow, or when either is removed. Start the planning with any part of your property where light conditions will not change.

- Wildlife interference is difficult to alter. Changes in your practices or plant selection can reduce wildlife interference, but, by and large, this is another "given."

- While overhead wires and underground pipes and cables could be moved in the future, they aren't likely to be. Look closely at these spots early on and decide how you will design, remembering that these obstructions are limiting factors.

- If you have windy spots, be sure to plant wind tolerant plants. Fortunately, most properties have calmer areas, as well.

- Where you site a new tree, shrub, woody vine or a garden for edibles or ornamentals, review (and possibly repeat) the visual observation activity to discover incriminating soil clods in Step 7 (Drainage), which alerts you to spots which

- You can remove, move, renew, or replace as many existing plants as you want to achieve your goals.

Making soil improvements is easier before planting than after. Add topsoil to lawn areas if necessary. For deeper-rooted plants (trees, shrubs, perennials, vegetables, fruit), incorporate organic matter into the top 1–3 feet of soil. When the pH is extremely different from what the new planting needs, it may be necessary to amend the soil a year before you plant.

Review the Landscape and Garden To-Do List sidebar below and make your to-do list. Then, come back to the text for advice on prioritizing tasks, plant selection, and sources for more information.

This barberry hedge can be easily renewed by pruning it to the ground resulting in new growth from the base.

Spading forks are easy-to-use tools for incorporating organic matter into existing soil before planting a new tree.

might have poor drainage. You may also wish to repeat the infiltration, percolation, and compaction tests in those spots, if you hadn't done so in the initial site assessment. Record results in your notebook.

In your notebook, make a list of site modifications you intend to make, if any. Here are some examples.

- You can correct a compaction or soil drainage issue. You may also choose to hardscape over a compacted area. There are few plantings that tolerate poor drainage or compacted soil.

- Where microclimates exist on your property, you can choose to adjust your plant selection to accommodate them.

- There are many topography changes you can make to allow you to plant on a steep slope.

Landscape and Garden To-Do List

The to-do list is an action plan for your property. You will need all the tools you developed: the Site Assessment Checklist, the property sketch, the plant inventory, maps of densely-planted areas, the draft landscape design, list of limitations, and notes taken during the site assessment. Many of the items that will go on the to-do list have already been identified. For example, unsafe areas were identified in Step 1.

The plant inventory includes notes on plants to be removed, moved, or renewed. Site modifications may have been identified throughout the process.

Record and date the to-do list in your site assessment notebook. Include a cost estimate for each task including contractor and/or materials cost. If you are doing the task yourself, estimate the number of hours it will take. Then, you can set reasonable expectations for implementing the design based on the time you have for the project. You can get more precise on cost and time required as you tackle the tasks.

Once the list is done, set priorities and review the completion dates to see if they are reasonable. Or, wait until the list is done to fill in dates based on your priorities.

Organize your to-do list using the categories below.

UNSAFE SPOTS TO FIX

Examples: level uneven spots in patio, driveway, or walkway; fill in depressions or holes in ground; remove short or broken pipes or other obstructions sticking up from ground; eradicate stinging insects; prune or remove trees with rotting or broken limbs; remove poison ivy, etc. Include the information below on your to-do list for each unsafe spot.

Unsafe condition _____

Location _____

Action _____

Hours required _____

Complete by _____

Estimated cost _____

SITE MODIFICATIONS TO BE MADE

Examples: build a patio; erect a pergola or trellis; install drainage pipes; install a retaining wall, terraces, or raised bed; build a fence; amend the soil; regrade a section; spread topsoil over a new lawn area; fill in a ground depression; change pathways; make the driveway narrower to make room for new planting on its edge, etc. Include the information below on your to-do list for each site modification.

Site modification _____

Location _____

Hours required _____

Complete by _____

Estimated cost _____

FATE OF EXISTING PLANTS

The plant inventory prepared in Step 11 has notes on the fate of existing plants. For each plant requiring an action, include the information below in your to-do list. The action could be remove, move, or renew. If a plant will be removed and you want to replace it, include "find replacement" or, if you have already decided, indicate the plant that will replace it. Include the new plant in the New Plantings to-do list. Only transfer plants from the inventory list if an action other than regular maintenance is planned.

Plant name and number _____

Location _____

Action _____

Hours required _____

Complete by _____

Estimated cost _____

NEW PLANTINGS

Determine the limitations of a new plantings location, if there are any. Examples of limitations include space, wet, dry, low soil pH, compacted soil, slopes, sunlight, underground utilities, overhead power lines, wind, frost pockets, reflected heat loads, rain shadows, rights-of-way, signs, outlets, vents, tree protection zones, etc.

A new planting may require additional tasks to make the location more favorable for the plant. You may need to adjust soil pH, correct compaction, fix drainage, block excessive wind, build a raised bed, amend soil in a planting bed with organic matter, fill in depression, rototill for new planting bed, install water outlet, install electrical outlet, etc.

Develop a list of new plantings based on the draft landscape design prepared earlier in this section. Include the information below for each new planting. For group plantings, prepare an entry for each type of plant.

Location _____

☐ Single Plant   ☐ Part of a Group Planting

Location Limitation _____

Plant selected _____

How many? _____

Additional tasks _____

Hours required _____

Complete by _____

Estimated cost _____

test determined there are elevated levels for a heavy metal, discuss options with garden participants. One option is to build raised beds and bring in soil without elevated heavy metal levels.

Then, start working on goals that will take months or years to achieve. Here are several examples:

■ If you need a windbreak planting, get an early start as it will take years before the trees mature enough to be effective.

■ If your plans include a plum, apple and/or pear tree orchard, get them sited and planted early on as they take several years to begin bearing fruit.

■ If a rhododendron planting would be beautiful to view from the dining room but the soil is not acid enough, start adjusting the soil pH six months to a year before planting. Postpone the rhododendron planting until the soil pH is acid enough. Also, consider plants more suitable to the soil characteristics such as an evergreen cherry laurel planting or a raised bed with soil that has the right pH.

■ If you want a shade tree near the master bedroom window, remember it will take years to create shade. However, don't jump immediately to planting the one on sale at the local garden

Digging into a steep slope to create terraces will reduce erosion.

Terraces result in better planting surfaces on the level ground above each wall.

Use your to-do list to help you prioritize — ranking what to do right away, what to do next year, and what can wait until you can afford the time and expense to do it. If you have an unlimited budget to hire outside labor, then your priority list might get done quite quickly. However, if you are like most of us, you will plan to do tasks related to construction, soil adjustment, and existing plants over a period of years as you can afford the time and expense to tackle them. Prioritizing is important to prevent you from tackling too much all at once.

First deal with construction or plant-related issues that are potential safety hazards to you, your family, or your guests. These areas are marked with an "H" on your sketch. You may have to do something as simple as repairing an uneven piece of brick walkway or something as drastic as removing an entire unsafe tree.

Address expensive construction changes as early as you can if they are critical to your goals. For instance, a series of terraces on a steep slope may be necessary because, without them, you continue to experience serious erosion problems. Erosion affects the landscape beyond the slope as well. Consider a temporary fix until you can afford the terraces.

If your site is a community garden where food plants will be grown and where a heavy metal soil center. Consider what your site assessment process revealed to you— soil, wind, hardiness, microclimates, drainage, wildlife, obstructions above and below, and all the other pertinent factors—to determine if the spot you prefer is right for a shade tree. You may need to make some site modifications. Prepare a short list of trees best suited for the spot before you start shopping.

- If you are covering a pergola over your patio with a woody vine such as wisteria, grape, or akebia, it will take several years to become established. Plant it early in your re-landscaping.

- If you must replace an undesirable or unsafe tree with one more appropriate for the location, the new tree will take several years to become established. Get an early start on this double project.

Using References and Resources

Reference books and websites mentioned throughout the workbook are invaluable tools to guide you through garden and landscape design and plant selection. Some of the references also address modification and maintenance. Add books to your home library if you will refer to them often, visit the local library to read others, and take advan-

tage of the wealth of information on the internet from reliable sources, such as the ones suggested throughout this workbook.

Human Factors

The emphasis in this workbook has been the importance of measured, observed, and tested information that you gather from the site. But gardens are designed, enjoyed, and used by people. There are human factors that will influence the goals and decisions made.

Human needs and wants sometimes don't want to wait until all the information is collected or the site is modified appropriately. For instance, sup-

pose that a homeowner has made the following two planting decisions:

- Decides that there must be a weeping beech tree, like the one he remembers fondly from his college campus. But in measuring the front yard, he finds that it is much smaller than the 500-square foot spread of a mature weeping beech tree. He also discovers that the water main comes in from the street in the front yard, where he wants the beech tree.

- Decides to plant blueberries. But, when he has the soil analyzed, he finds that his soil is not acid enough for blueberries.

If the homeowner plants the beech tree and blueberries anyway, he will struggle for years with them. He must first realize that the tree, as it matures, will not fit in the front yard and he has to conclude that any tree on top of a water main is a poor landscape choice. Herbaceous perennials, shrubs, and lawns are easier to dig up and replant if the water main needs repair. In addition, he must realize that soil modification to adjust the pH is critical for productive blueberry plants. Otherwise, the blueberry yield will suffer and, in the long run, the plants will become yellowish, skimpy, and unattractive.

Bradford callery pear trees are weak wooded and easily damaged by storms, especially as they mature. This tree should be removed.

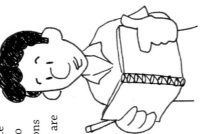

Pete's curious neighbor George comments on the site assessment.

If there is a public garden (botanic(al) garden, arboretum) in your area, check to see if they provide gardening advice, particularly on the environmental needs of plants or questions about existing plants. Visiting a public garden may help you visualize your landscape and garden goals, especially the plants you want to include.

Neighbors may be a source of advice but you will need to differentiate between opinions and good information. They are a source of information on factors the neighborhood shares, like wind and roaming animals.

To assist you in doing research on landscape design and plant selection, there is a list of references and resources in the pages that follow.

Be like Pete and his dog Herb by taking a moment to sit back and enjoy what you have discovered and what lies ahead in creating unique and environmentally-friendly outdoor spaces.

Human determination is a good thing, but sometimes it gets in the way of what good gardening requires—the right plant in the right place.

Or how about the human desire to have a perfect green carpet of a lawn like a neighbor's? A home owner discovers a 100-square-foot area next to the garage where the soil is compacted. She tries different kinds of grass seed, but it never takes hold. She invests in pre-grown sod to roll out for an instantly green lawn, but after a few years, the sod kind of peters out as well. She hasn't addressed the source of the problem—compaction. Modifying the site by mitigating the compaction may be her only option.

Another human fact of life is the influence of others. What is abundant for most of us are suggestions from family, friends, and neighbors, as well as magazine articles and gardening catalogs with alluring photos. You may desire to recreate elements and features from gardens and landscapes seen in other places. Your site assessment results will help you rationally accept or reject these ideas.

Finally, what are your preferences? If you have always wanted an herb garden, for instance, and your site assessment indicates you have a location with loamy, well-drained soil and six hours of sunlight, make it a high priority in the to-do list. Start there with a garden design. Begin to enjoy your outdoor environment and the pleasure of gardening. If you find yourself saying that you want it all right away, sit back, realize that it may not be possible, and develop a reasonable timeline to achieve your goals.

Where do I get advice, if I need it?

Throughout the book, sources of advice were mentioned including local Cooperative Extension offices. Cooperative Extension may be a good source of information on local climate, plants that thrive in the area, soil testing labs, gardening classes, and state level horticulture experts. Cooperative Extension is a nationwide education system that originally had offices in each U.S county. In some states, multi-county offices have replaced county offices. Local offices are linked to the state's land grant university. Some states have local gardening education programs supported by horticultural experts at the state's land grant university. Other states may not offer this service.

Utility companies provide information on underground conduits and overhead wires. Soil and water conservation districts provide information on local soils and wetland rules if needed. Using the books and websites mentioned in this book, you can find information on all aspects of landscape and gardens. Professional landscape architects can be good consultants for problematic areas.

PLANTS MENTIONED IN TAKING THE NEXT STEPS

The common name is followed by the scientific name and then additional information if needed.

Akebia – *Akebia quinata*

Apple – *Malus domestica*. There are over 7,500 known cultivars of apple.

Barberry (red-leaved) – *Berberis thunbergii* variety *atropurpurea*

Boxwood – *Buxus* sp. – a genus of over 70 species; the most common is *Buxus sempervirens*.

Bradford Callery Pear – *Pyrus calleryana* 'Bradford'

Cherry laurel – *Prunus laurocerasus*

Grape – *Vitis* sp. – a genus of about 60 species and many more cultivars and hybrids.

Pete and Herb satisfied with their new landscape.

Pear – *Pyrus* sp. Several species and many more cultivars are grown for edible fruit; others are grown as ornamental trees.

Plum – *Prunus* sp. – a genus of more than 20 species and more cultivars. *Prunus domestica* is the species of most plums and prunes.

Rhododendron – *Rhododendron* sp. – a genus of more than 900 species, which includes plants with the common names of azalea and rhododendron. When used as a common name, rhododendron refers to shrubs with large clusters of flowers.

Weeping beech tree – *Fagus sylvatica* 'Pendula', a cultivar of European beech

Wisteria – *Wisteria* sp. – a genus of about 8 species. The most common are *Wisteria sinensis* (Chinese wisteria), *Wisteria floribunda* (Japanese wisteria) and *Wisteria frutescens* (American wisteria)

References and Resources

Visit **http://www.hort.cornell.edu/site/** *for links to the web sites below and all web sites mentioned in this book.*

GENERAL ADVICE

Botanical Gardens, Public Gardens, and Arboretum Locations

http://gardenvisit.com/gardens/in/usa
From Nightingale Garden Company, Ltd., registered in England and Wales.

http://www.garden.org/publicgarden
From the National Gardening Association.

Cooperative Extension Office Locations

http://www.csrees.usda.gov/Extension/
From the United States Department of Agriculture.

Home and Garden Information Center

http://extension.umd.edu/hgic

Horticultural information for the public nationwide through a diagnostic website. By the University of Maryland Cooperative Extension.

LANDSCAPE DESIGN

Land grant university Cooperative Extension programs provide resources that can help you adapt this workbook to your region. Consult your state's Cooperative Extension service and/or county office for specific local information. Here are a few:

Developing a Landscape Plan, from the University of Missouri, Reviewed by David H. Trinklein. View this online at: **http://extension.missouri.edu/xplor/agguides/hort/g06901.htm**

Home Landscape: Understanding the Basics of Landscape Design, from the University of Nebraska. To order a copy, visit **http://www.ianrpubs.unl.edu/sendIt/ec1254.html.**

Landscape Rejuvenation: Remodeling the Home Landscape, by Dr. Bonnie Lee Appleton, Storey Publications, North Adams, Massachusetts,

1988. (Out-of-print, available in libraries, used bookstores, and through online booksellers.)

Planning and Designing Your Home Landscape, from the University of Wisconsin. To order a paper copy or view a PDF copy, go to: **http://learningstore.uwex.edu/Planning-and-Designing-Your-Home-Landscape-P754.aspx**

Landscaping Your Home, by William R. Nelson, Jr., University of Illinois at Urbana-Champaign College of Agriculture, 1975. Available through online booksellers.

PLANT SELECTION

These references include a few that are mentioned earlier in the workbook.

Hardy Trees and Shrubs: An Illustrated Encyclopedia, by Michael A. Dirr, Timber Press, Portland, Oregon 1997. Useful for its abundant photographs, but not as comprehensive as Dirr's *Manual of Woody Landscape Plants* listed on page 70.

Herbaceous Perennial Plants: A Treatise on Their Identification, Culture, and Garden Attributes, by Allan M. Armitage, Varsity Press, Athens, Georgia, 1989.

Improve Your Soil with Cover Crops, Ecogardening Factsheet #9 **http://blogs.cornell.edu/horticulture/about/basic-gardening-info/cover-crops/** From Cornell Garden Based Learning, the Department of Horticulture, Cornell University.

Lawn Care for Dummies, by Lance Walheim, National Gardening Association, Hungry Minds Inc., New York, 1998.

Manual of Woody Landscape Plants, 6th Edition, by Michael Dirr, Stipes Publishing, LLC, Champaign, Illinois, 2009.

Plant Database of Trees, Shrubs and Vines, University of Connecticut. Trees, shrubs, and vines are listed by common and scientific name along with plant attributes. **www.hort.uconn.edu/plants/**

Plants for Problem Spaces, by Graham Rice, Timber Press, Portland, Oregon, 1988.

Recommended Urban Trees: Site Assessment and Tree Selection for Stress Tolerance, Urban Horticulture Institute, Cornell University, 2009. Available online in PDF format at: **http://www.hort.cornell.edu/uhi/outreach/recurbtree/** This site also includes an order form for a 133-page paper copy.

Tough Plants for Tough Places, by Gary Vergine and Michael Jefferson-Brown, Contemporary Books, Lincolnwood, Illinois, 1998.

Tree ID Guide for Common Urban Trees in New York State and the Northeast. From the Urban Horticulture Institute, Department of Horticulture, at Cornell University. Order form available for this pocket-sized book at: **http://www.hort.cornell.edu/uhi/outreach/index.htm**

Trees and Shrubs for Warm Climates: An Illustrated Encyclopedia, by Michael A. Dirr, Timber Press 2002. Useful for its abundant photographs, but not as comprehensive as Dirr's *Manual of Woody Landscape Plants* listed above.

What Perennial Where, by Roy Lancaster, DK Publishing, London, 1997.

GROWING VEGETABLES AND FRUITS

Cornell Gardening Resources—Vegetables, Cornell University **http://blogs.cornell.edu/horticulture/vegetables/** The Cornell site has a vegetable selection feature, while most other sources only tell you how to grow a particular vegetable. Consult your local Cooperative Extension for vegetable gardening information suitable for your region.

Cornell Guide to Growing Fruit at Home, Department of Horticulture, Cornell University, 2003. Includes sections on tree fruits, grapes, strawberries, brambles, blueberries, and more. **www.gardening.cornell.edu/fruit/homefruit.html**

Encyclopedia of Organic Gardening, by the staff of Organic Gardening and Farming Magazine, Rodale Books, Inc., Emmaus, Pennsylvania, 1999.

Home Vegetable Gardening, by Larry Bass, North Carolina State University **www.ces.ncsu.edu/depts/hort/hil/ag-06.html**

Glossary

Air circulation (good) – a condition where the air flows freely through the plants. Air circulates through and around the plants throughout the day; the air is not stagnant and air movement is not impeded by walls, a mass of tall plants (such as shrubs), or other obstructions. Good air circulation minimizes disease.

Amending – in gardening, adding materials (amendments) such as sand, organic matter, perlite, vermiculite, or crushed stone to the soil.

Animal pressure – often expressed as low, medium, or high when discussing a specific animal (for example high deer pressure). The degree of pressure reflects both the number of animals and the animals' dependency on the garden for food. In areas with high pressure, animals are less discriminating in their vegetation choices and more difficult to deter.

Annual flowers – See *Annuals* below.

Annuals – plants that complete their life cycle from seed to flower to fruit in one growing season. Some plants, grown as perennials in warmer climates, are grown as annuals in colder climates because they can not survive the cold winter temperatures. Annuals usually refer to flowers but there are also annual vegetables and annual herbs.

Arboretum – a collection of trees, shrubs, and woody vines in a public garden. See also *Botanic garden* in this glossary

Balcony garden – a balcony where plants are grown, usually in containers. See also *Terrace* in this glossary.

Bed – a place in a garden or landscape where many plants are grown.

Botanic garden (or botanical garden) – a public garden devoted to education, conservation, and plant display. Some include an area exclusively for trees, shrubs, and woody vines (called an arboretum). Botanical gardens usually have labeled plants or reference maps to help you learn what plants are on the grounds.

See also *Arboretum* in this glossary.

Breast height, tree diameter (dbh) – a measurement made at 4.5 feet above ground on mature trees. The circumference is measured. The diameter is the circumference divided by 3.14.

Broad-leaved evergreens – plants, such as rhododendron and holly, which retain wide leaves (not narrow needled leaves) throughout the year, including winter. See *Evergreens* and *Deciduous* in this glossary. *See photo on page 48.*

Browse line – the line below which deer or other animals have eaten most of a plant's green parts. *See photo on page 47.*

Bubble level – an instrument designed to indicate whether a surface is level or plumb using a floating bubble. *See drawing on page 41.*

Burlap – a brown-coarse fabric used to cover plants and protect them against excessive winds, snow, or ice. *See photo on page 24.*

Caliper – tree diameter measured 6 inches above the ground if the diameter is less than 4 inches or at 12 inches above ground if the diameter is over 4 inches. Caliper is used by nurseries to describe trees for sale.

Cell – the basic living unit in any plant (or animal). Contains a nucleus, protoplasm, vital small organs (organelles), a membrane, and, in plants, a wall.

Circumference (tree) – the distance around a circle or cylinder, such as a tree. Circumference divided by 3.14 equals the tree diameter.

Clay – an essential part of most soils that is efficient in holding reserve minerals needed by the plant for nutrition. Clay particles are miniscule in size, but they clump together into aggregates, and their individual small size is often obscured. Too much clay in soil can restrict drainage. See *Drainage* in this glossary. Also refers to a soil textural class. *See diagram on page 36. See USDA Soil Textural Class Triangle* in this glossary.

Clayey – soil having a heavy, gummy consistency.

Community garden – a shared garden space for community members owned privately or by a municipality and located in a neighbor-hood or a commonly accessible place. Often characterized by plots, managed by individuals. A common space for the entire group to manage, gather, and have shared events may be included. Policy decisions are usually made by a committee of participants. *See photos on page 2 and 26.*

Compacted soil – soil whose pores are crushed and air squeezed out due to activity on the soil surface. It is hard to dig and hard for roots to grow in this soil. *See photo on page 26.*

Compost – In gardening, a soil amendment used to improve soil structure and provide nutrients. Compost, an organic matter, results from a process where organic residues are mixed in proportions that encourage accelerated decomposition. The organic residues are altered in the process. Compost is abundant with microorganisms and, often, worms – both of which are assets to the garden. Compost sold at garden centers may be from either plant or animal origin. At home, plant materials are usually used to make compost. See *Organic matter* and *Microorganisms* in this glossary.

Cover crops – plants sown from seed over a wide swath of space in a vegetable garden to improve the condition of the soil. Examples of cover crops include annual ryegrass, winter rye, winter wheat, oats, white clover, sweet clover, hairy vetch, and buckwheat.

Cultivar – cultivated variety. A term that differentiates plant species based on noticeable factors such as flower color, vegetable yield, plant size, or other factors. Winter hardiness and disease resistance, which are not readily apparent, can also vary among cultivars of the same plant.

Deciduous (tree) – Loses leaves in the fall with new ones emerging each spring.

Deicing salts – see *Road salt.*

Design, landscape and/or garden – a purposeful arrangement of plants, paths, benches, statues, and other garden features described with a drawing. A draft design is drawn first and refined as more information becomes available. It begins the final stage of laying out where you want elements of the future landscape and gardens to be located. See also *Property sketch* in this glossary.

Diameter (tree) – a measure of the tree's size and maturity. Diameter is a straight line across the circular shape of the tree trunk, passing through the center and reaching both ends.

Radius is one half of the diameter. *See photos on page 53 and page 54. See Breast height, Caliper,* and *Circumference* in this glossary.

Disease organisms – microscopic living cells from a fungus, bacteria, or virus that cause disease in a plant (or animal).

Disease – a condition in plants that is caused by a fungus, bacteria, or virus. Disease damage is usually different than damage by insects, but frequently there are similar symptoms, such as wilting or discoloration. *See photo of Austrian Pine on page 51. See also Insects (garden),* in this glossary.

Draft landscape design – see *Design, Landscape and/or garden*

Drainage – Movement of irrigation or rain water through the topsoil and subsoil. In soils with poor drainage, water drains slowly limiting oxygen available to roots. In a well-drained soil, excess water easily moves through the subsoil leaving pores with both water and oxygen. *See photos on page 29.*

Drought resistant – able to withstand long periods in a dry habitat. There is a genetic basis to the wide variation in plants' ability to withstand days or weeks in a landscape without watering.

Erosion (soil) – the process of soil washing or blowing away from the surface.

Evergreens – plants that retain their leaves in the winter. They may be needled evergreens (for example pine, spruce, fir) or broad-leaved evergreens (for example rhododendron, cherry laurel, holly)

Fertilize – adding nutrients to supplement nutrients available in the soil.

Frost dates – the dates when frost is most likely to stop occurring in the spring and begin occurring in the fall.

Frost pockets – outdoor places where cold air collects. These areas may freeze before the surrounding area. *See photo on page 18.*

Garden center – a retail store that specializes in selling plants and garden supplies. See *Nursery* in this glossary.

Garden design – see *Design, landscape and/or garden.*

Gardens – in-ground or containerized, edible or ornamental plants in a formal or informal design. Often the term garden is used generically to include landscaped areas of trees, shrubs, and ground covers. See *Landscapes (cultivated).*

Girdling roots – tree roots that circle at the base of the trunk. They may be caused by compacted soil, too-deep planting, poor drainage, and/or improper planting. It has been observed that trees planted from containers, where the roots, which began circling in the round pot, can develop girdling roots. The young circling roots mature and cause greater force against the trunk. In some cases, this leads to its decline and death in later years. *See photo on page 52.*

Gradient – The change in elevation between two points divided by the horizontal distance between the two points. Also referred to as grade.

Grid-lined paper – paper covered with uniformly sized, tiny blocks (or grids). Useful in making sketches and landscape/garden designs to scale.

Ground covers – plants of one species and variety used en mass to cover a large area. The plants are generally herbaceous perennials, including broad leaved or ornamental grass plants, and shrubs. They may be a few inches high to a few feet high, but are relatively uniform in height to create a carpet or understory effect. Ground covers are generally intended to be permanent to the landscape, although a temporary ground cover of annual plants might be used while more permanent plants get established. Lawn is also a ground cover, but the term usually refers to plants other than lawn grasses in the landscape.

Growing season – in a four-season climate, growing tends to span from April to October, more or less in hotter or colder areas. Growth does not occur in the colder months of winter, late fall or early spring.

Growth rate – the rate at which a plant grows. It is influenced by genetics, cultural practices, and the environment. *See Tree Growth Rate sidebar on page 55.*

Hardiness – in gardening, it refers to a plant's ability to overwinter, meaning it will survive through the lowest winter temperatures. *See map on page 17.*

Hardscaping – replacing grass or soil with stone, brick, paving, or other non-plant material. A hardscape addition may be made where it is difficult to grow plants successfully, due to compacted or poorly-drained soil. Paths, driveways and patios are examples of hardscape additions for personal preference or need. *See photos on page 28.*

Herbs – plants with a practical use, including culinary, medicinal, cosmetic, fabric dying, or in some cases, a spiritual use. Can be annuals or perennials.

Herbaceous perennials – plants that die back to the ground every fall and re-emerge in the spring with new stem and leaf growth. Roots persist throughout the winter. Sometimes casually referred to as perennials, even though, technically, some perennials are herbaceous and others are woody. *See Woody plants in this glossary.*

Herbaceous plant – a plant whose stems are soft or fibrous and die back every year. Both annuals and perennials can be herbaceous. See *Herbaceous perennials*, *Annuals*, and *Herbs.*

Infiltration – Movement of water into the soil surface. Infiltration rates are described as poor, moderate, good, or excessive.

Insects (garden) – a class of beneficial and harmful organisms. Some are beneficial in pollination (e.g. honey bees) or because they eat harmful insects (e.g. lady bugs); others, called pests, do harm by chewing plant parts (e.g. slugs) or sucking juices (e.g. aphids) which weaken plants. Insects can be seen in the egg, larval, nymph, pupal or adult stages. *See photo on page 51.* See also *Disease* in this glossary.

Irrigation system – pump, filter, pipes, and emitters or sprinklers installed to deliver water to plants.

Landscape design – see *Design, Landscape and/or garden.*

Landscapes (cultivated) – those planted areas that contain mostly woody trees and shrubs, as well as herbaceous ground covers and often clumps of herbaceous perennials and flowering annuals. See *Gardens* in this glossary.

Lime – any of several forms of calcium used for improving soil that has low calcium content. Lime raises the soil pH.

Loam – a soil that contains roughly equal portions of sand and silt with slightly less clay. Defined as soil that contains less than 52% sand, 28 to 50% silt, and 7 to 27% clay. Also refers to a soil textural class. *See diagram on page 36. See USDA Soil Textural Class Triangle in this glossary.*

Loamy – In gardening, used to describe a soil that retains moisture and drains well.

Maintenance – the care of plants after site assessment and planting. Examples of maintenance are fertilizing, pruning, staking, winter protection, mulching, disease management, and many more.

Map – In this book, a drawing of an area where the plants are too numerous and close together to tag them when making a plant inventory.

Marginal leaf scorch – a symptom of plant damage where the edges of the leaves are brown; could be caused by disease, drought, or salt uptake. *See photo on page 52.*

Maturity – the stage where a plant reaches its full size. For trees and shrubs, maturity is reached when annual growth is slow or imperceptible.

Microclimate – an area where the climate differs from the surrounding area. The term may refer to areas as small as a few square feet (e.g. a garden bed) or as large as many square miles (e.g. a valley). *See photos on page 18, page 19, and page 22.*

Microorganisms – living things that are usually too small to be seen without a microscope. They include bacteria and fungi.

Mulch – a layer of organic (e.g. tree bark, straw, or plant hulls) or inorganic (e.g. stones, plastic sheets) material that covers the soil and helps minimize weed growth and water loss.

Noxious weeds – unwanted plants that multiply rapidly and are difficult to eradicate. They are called invasive when the origin of the species is exotic meaning non-native. Invasive weeds adversely affect habitats of native plant communities. *See photos on page 55.*

Nursery – a retail or wholesale business that specializes in growing plants for resale. See also *Garden Center* in this glossary.

Organic matter (soil) – decomposed plant or animal matter that conditions the soil, making it healthier and more welcoming to microorganisms. Organic matter improves water-holding capacity and resistance to compaction. Examples include compost and peat moss.

Percolation – the movement of water into the subsoil under near saturated conditions. Percolation rates are described as poor, moderate, or excessive. See *Drainage* in this glossary.

Perennials – Perennials refer to plants that survive through the winter and come back each year. See *Herbaceous perennials, Vines,* and *Woody plants* in this glossary.

Pergola – a structure which forms a shaded sitting area or walkway, made up of vertical posts, horizontal beams. Woody vines weave through the open framework as they grow.

pH – the measure, on a scale of 0–14, of acidity or alkalinity of the soil. A soil characteristic that influences whether a plant will succeed in an area. *See diagram on page 37.*

Plant inventory – in this book, a list of plants growing on the property.

Pores (soil) or **pore spaces** – essential space between soil particles.

Pores (leaves) – tiny, almost invisible openings that allow gases, like oxygen, carbon dioxide and water vapor to enter or exit the leaves. Technically called stomates or stomata.

Property sketch – in this workbook, it refers to a simple drawing showing the layout of the property being assessed. Included are dimensions, obstructions, light exposure, and other factors. It is ideally drawn to scale. For example, 1 inch on the sketch equals 50 feet on the site. See also *Design, landscape and/or garden* in this glossary.

Property survey – found in a deed and drawn by a surveyor to scale to show property lines, dimensions, rights-of-way, buildings and other permanent structures as well as other significant elements of a piece of private or public property. *See drawing on page 7.*

Pruning – the act of cutting plant parts (mostly stems) to improve the health of the plant or to reshape it.

Rain shadows – places under the eaves of buildings where rain cannot easily reach the plants underneath. Rain shadows can also exist on one side of a solid fence or wall, or under a tree. In some cases, a row of shrubs, high and dense enough to block blowing wind, may result in a rain shadow on one side. *See photo on page 19.*

Raised bed – a planting area in which the soil level is elevated above ground level, usually no more than 1–3 feet; a raised bed is constructed with wood, while a raised mound does not have sidewalls.

Renew (plants) – prune, fertilize, treat for disease, or eliminate harmful insect collections (such as tent caterpillar egg masses); generally, bring the plant into a healthy condition and improve it for the landscape or garden. *See photo on page 62.*

Reflected heat load – an area with heat pockets due to reflected and radiated heat from pavement, automobiles, buildings, or other surfaces. This can cause trees to heat up and lose water from their leaves at a faster-than-normal rate. These pockets often face south and retain a tremendous amount of heat. On sunny days, these areas will be noticeably warmer than nearby spots. *See photo on page 18.*

Road salt – various chemical substances applied to streets and roads to reduce slippery conditions for cars and pedestrians during winter. Salts are combinations of chemical elements, such as calcium, sodium, chlorine, and sulfur. Most do harm to plant roots and aboveground plant parts if they are concentrated in melting snow/ice and splash onto the plants and soil. Rain may also wash salted water from streets and roads into roots. *See Soluble salts.*

Roots – below ground plant parts. Roots support the plant. Fine roots absorb nutrients from the soil which are transported to the rest of the plant. Roots also store starches over the winter that are available to perennial plants for early spring growth. *See Girdling roots and Surface rooting.*

Rootstock – The bottom part of a tree with a healthy root system, used for grafting another tree with desirable characteristics, such as fruit flavor, onto it. Dwarfing rootstocks are used often for fruit trees to render the desirable tree, grafted on top, less tall than it would normally be. The dwarfing characteristic comes about because of chemical interactions between the rootstock and the top grafted tree (called the scion).

Sand – an important component of many soil types, composed of silicon dioxide, also known as silica. It allows drainage, but has little to no ability to retain nutrients by itself. *See Drainage* in this glossary. Also refers to a soil textural class. *See diagram on page 36. See USDA Soil Textural Class Triangle* in this glossary.

Sandy – used to describe a soil that has a large sand component.

Shrub – a plant with multiple woody stems. Shrubs can range from less than a foot tall to over 10 feet tall, with sparse or dense branching. They differ from trees by having multiple branches coming from the base. *See Woody plants* in this glossary.

Silt – soil particles that are intermediate in size (smaller than sand and larger than clay the result of neglect, poor drainage, too-deep planting, and/or compacted soil or a harmful condition, such as erosion. These conditions can cause roots to grow near the surface, making the tree less sturdy. *See photo on page 52. See Roots in this glossary.*

Sustainable – in this book, it refers to collecting information on the opportunities and limitations of the site so that decisions will result in reduced plant stress and an easy-to-care-for garden.

Terrace – used in two different ways in this workbook:

1. an area outside a building where container gardens are typically located. Terraces can be on the ground (as in a patio) or aboveground (as in a balcony). The term can also be extended to mean rooftop container gardens.

2. flat planting areas above low retaining walls (or terrace walls). Terraces form a series of "steps" on a slope. Plants are set into the flat area to increase roots' ability to become established without erosion. *See photos on page 42 and page 65.*

Texture (soil) – the relative proportion of clay, sand, and silt in soil *See photo on page 35 and*

Stress factors – inadequate or excessive environmental conditions in landscapes and gardens, such as oxygen, water, light, nutrients, carbon dioxide, and temperature.

String trimmer – power equipment that cuts grass or weeds along edges in the landscape. Improper use can damage tree trunks and shrubs. Also known as a weed wacker.

Study area – in this workbook, an area within the site where intensive data is collected for decision making. It is distinguished from a property's site assessment in being focused on a smaller area, such as an alcove or area where changes are expected.

Subsoil – the soil under the topsoil. It usually contains less organic matter than top soil and nutrients are less available. In growing plants, much depends on the ability of water to pass through the subsoil. If flow is restricted, the pore spaces around the roots can be filled with water limiting oxygen availability. See *Drainage.*

Surface rooting – when roots of trees and shrubs are visible on the surface of the soil. Sometimes it is the result of the genetic capacity of the plant, such as beech trees, which usually have surface roots. Sometimes it is

---

particles). Also refers to a soil textural class. *See diagram on page 36. See USDA Soil Textural Class Triangle in this glossary.*

Silty – used to describe a soil that is mostly silt particles.

Site modification – making changes to a site to meet the needs of the plants, for human interests, or to prevent erosion. *See diagrams on page 1 and page 60.*

Sketch – See *property sketch* in this glossary.

Slope – used to describe land that is not level. Also, the change in elevation over a horizontal distance, expressed as a percent. Specifically, the change in elevation, divided by the horizontal distance, multiplied by 100. *See photo on page 40 and drawing on page 41.*

Soluble salts – combinations of inorganic elements that can, when in excess, burn plant roots. See *Road salt.*

Stabilizing – used to describe plants whose root structure can stabilize a slope and prevent erosion.

Storage device, digital – computer, flash, or thumb drive, camera memory card, smart phone, digital tablet, or other electronic devices to store information and photos.

diagram on page 36. See USDA Soil Textural Class Triangle in this glossary.

Tip dieback – a disease that manifests itself by growth or death at the tips of many branches. The disease progresses and can be referred to as dieback in its more advanced stages.

Topography – the slope and lay of the land. The configuration of a surface including its elevation changes, depressions, and low-lying areas and the position of its natural and man-made features.

Topsoil – the uppermost layer of soil, usually the top 2 to 6 inches. See *Subsoil* in this glossary.

Transplanting – the practice of moving plants from one location to another. Site assessment may lead a property owner to transplant a tree, shrub, or herbaceous perennial to a location better suited to the plants' needs.

Tree – a plant with a wood trunk and branches. It is distinguished from a shrub (which also has woody branches) by usually having only one trunk. See *Woody plants.*

Trellising – supporting vertical growth of a vine with wooden, metal, or plastic stakes, usually in a decorative form.

USDA Soil Textural Class Triangle – A precise, scientific classification of twelve distinct soil types, as defined by the United States Depart-

ment of Agriculture (USDA). This diagram is referred to and useful to soil scientists and for those reading books or websites that refer to it.

Vines – plants that have a growth habit of climbing or trailing. Climbing vines use other plants or supports to grow upward. Trailing vines grow along the ground. They may be annual or perennial, herbaceous or woody. See *Annuals, Herbaceous perennials,* and *Woody plants.*

Windbreaks – wind-resistant trees or shrubs that block the wind creating a calm area and protecting wind sensitive plants.

Woody plants – perennial plants (trees, shrubs, and vines) that develop an abundance of a hard substance called lignin in their cell walls to form woody stems. The stems (trunks and branches that grow thicker each year) are firm and remain on the plant throughout the winter. Woody plants can be deciduous (dropping their leaves in the winter) or evergreen (retaining leaves through the winter—broad or needle). See also *Herbaceous plants.*

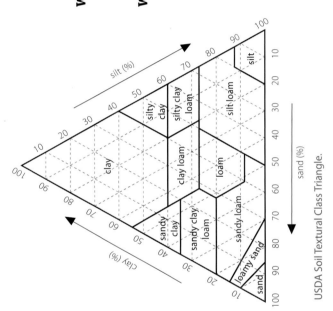

USDA Soil Textural Class Triangle.

Index

Bolded numbers indicate pages with photos or illustrations related to the term. The text on that page may also include the term.

79